Published by Semiotext(e)
PO BOX 629, South Pasadena, CA 91031
www.semiotexte.com

Special thanks to John Ebert and Janique Vigier.

Cover Art: Josephine Pryde, *Sorry Not Sorry*, 2016.
Design: Hedi El Kholti

ISBN: 978-1-63590-096-5

Distributed by The MIT Press, Cambridge, Mass. and London, England
Printed in the United States of America

10 9 8 7 6 5 4 3

Sleeveless

Fashion, Image, Media, New York 2011–2019

Natasha Stagg

semiotext(e)

Contents

Foreword

Since publishing my first novel, *Surveys*, I've been placed in the unique position of being asked to think about its implications as they evolve around me. *Surveys* is a coming-of-age story, but its central themes are jealousy, fame, and statistics, and its release coincided with an explosion of new terms that better define and obfuscate those themes as felt today. The word "influencer" has a different meaning than it did while I was writing a character that many reviews have named an "influencer," for example.

New ways of branding, and of defining branded interactions, are unquestionably informing the ways in which we think. In other words, it is ever more difficult to imagine ourselves the way we once did, before we were made to feel so implicit in advertising.

I started to write these essays and stories upon moving to New York in 2011. They were inspired by my jobs here, mostly, but also by my friends: their jobs, their joblessness in the face of career paths being redefined by digital marketing, their incidental or planned star statuses, and their waning popularity. I've learned valuable lessons from meeting and interviewing my idols, dating my celebrity crush, getting put on a thousand press lists, slipping in and out of literary and fashion spheres, contributing to publications I care about, and watching print media devolve. It's fun to talk about certain New York things once being better than they are now, as if I can really claim something like that.

These entries—some fiction, some not—are not presented in chronological order, because once I started to organize them, I saw that the perspective I held back then was perhaps more clear-sighted than the one I have today. Right now, I write more advertorial work than anything else, and that means that I participate in a structure that inhibits my own creative writing while informing it. Every day, I must think about advertising strategies based on a quickly changing consumer landscape. I must gauge my own ideas of individuality, persona, and authenticity, while I internally negotiate the monetization of my generation, my identity, my space, myself. I critique fashion and I also work for fashion brands. I write about the processes of promotion and I also write ad copy. I'm skeptical of the influencer epidemic and the popularity of my writing puts me at risk of becoming influential. At times, consumerism's close breath feels like fresh air.

And so, the following is a collection of thoughts about fashion, perception, publishing, image-making, gender biases, and reputation, from inside the think tanks about those things. If I look at it in a dystopian way, this might be the last chance I have to thoughtfully speak on these subjects, before I forget them, like a dream, because of their very own projections. I'd rather see this book as a personal account of a very strange time, though, and an attempt to identify the invisible strings pulling us in directions we never thought possible.

Public Relations

Cafeteria

They meet at Cafeteria because the characters in *Sex and the City* did that. The New York of that era is not the same as the New York of today, but even while the show aired, viewers argued that it wasn't of a real New York. So the collective city—the idea that became known as another main character, which was New York in quotes, or female friendship, or whatever was under your nose the whole time—is as real as anything on TV, and therefore hasn't changed.

The group of friends is two men who have been dating for some time, a woman who has known them each for longer, and a recent transplant to the city who met the other three two weeks ago—a guy each member of the group would like to fuck.

The week is New York Fashion Week Fall 2012, which happens in icy February but people are wearing the Spring collections. It's early but everyone orders tequila cocktails. The menu boasts that Cafeteria is a haven for the stars of New York nightlife, the ones who still get name checked in magazine stories, effusively described as "legendary," the original versions of the new somethings.

In the days of interview expense accounts, said one of the friends, a journalist would take a club kid out all day and get trashed, making sure the story only described how magnetic and charismatic this person was—the world was her oyster type things. But the writer got something out of this, too. The scam was that the parties were cooler because they were getting written up, while the writers were getting to go to the coolest parties because they had the power to make them so.

That was when parties were cool.

Parties are still cool, said the recent transplant. I went to a cool one last night. I'm still kind of fucked up from it, oh my god.

Getting fucked up is cool, said the woman.

Never won't be, will it?

I can see it going out of style.

I was sitting at an adjacent table, eavesdropping and looking at my laptop. I caught a few names and ended up finding all of them. The woman was a curator, the two men music producers, and the younger man worked at a second-hand store. They talked about how none of them ever wanted to be famous, how they were disappointed by a recent collaboration between an artist famous for critiquing capitalist values and Topshop, and how broke they all were.

I didn't know of that artist or which lower-rung nightlife stars they were avoiding eye contact with in the booth across the restaurant, or whether, when they said interview expense, accounts they'd meant the magazine, *Interview*. In the days of interview accounts, though, they said, everything could be expensed, including helicopters to the Hamptons. I guessed that every single one of them wanted to be stars, with the sky as the limit.

I saved all of their information and waited until the next day to email one of them, starting with the curator. I know now that I was correct and that I am closer to all of them for it. I understand that the best thing to be in New York is watched and heard, and that if those chats around cosmos in the TV show weren't written for an audience, they wouldn't be so optimistic. No character was doing so well that the city could feel like a supportive friend to her. You can't move here and expect to be able to live the way the locals do, relaxing into their adult lives, frequenting their favorite Manhattan haunts, maintaining deep-rooted friendships. Instead, the best you can hope for is to make friends who make time for you, and who would not disagree when you publicized your closeness. Would they put you on a guest list? Depends.

The curator was kind and opened up to me quickly. She couldn't wait to meet me and to introduce me to the artists she worked with. She had been to the part of New Jersey where my family was from because she'd been a last minute date to a wedding there. She loved it, she said.

The parties in New York, I told the group, they could still be good, as long as they're sponsored well. Yes, they said, and who cares about a little advertising? They are my friends now. I am their publicist.

Two Stops

November 6, 2017

The after-party for the Calvin Klein Underwear exhibition was held on one of the piers, I forget which one. I couldn't even tell if we were in Brooklyn or Manhattan, because we'd been driven to the venue in a bus with tinted windows. The party's centerpiece was a performance by Kesha, but she cancelled last minute. Now that we didn't have to watch her perform, we had an excuse to say we were fans.

There were free drinks at the bar, and waiters kept coming by with hors d'oeuvres. My date, B, was an intern I'd met a few months earlier at another sponsored party. Since then I'd learned that he was into threesomes, didn't work in fashion or PR, and didn't have Instagram. He was from Switzerland and new to America and refused to tell me his age. Whenever we were together it was hard to tell what would happen between us: nothing, something, or something crazy. I wondered if my friends thought I looked too old for him.

I knew B liked to flirt at parties, but that night, every time he shook someone's hand, he put his arm around me and held me closer. He kissed me softly on the cheek, a more tender gesture than I was used to. I watched as he flirted with gay men while making sure they knew he was joking—he would never! Especially not that night, when he was with me. This was offensive, the way B would always tell men he'd make exceptions for each of them, except that he wouldn't. Would he?

I talked to my old coworkers about their new jobs and about our old boss, an awful man who would never get called out for his misconduct. Some of us had seen him on dates with the male models he brought around to the office, but we didn't know for sure that he'd slept with them.

We talked about other editors we knew were cruel and sleazy, about fashion photographers who should have been jailed long ago. A couple of weeks earlier, Condé Nast had announced they were no longer working with Terry Richardson, but by that point the allegations against him were many years old. One editor at the party seemed uncomfortable talking about any of it, maybe because his magazine featured Terry's work all the time.

B handed me a champagne flute.

"We're talking about sexual misconduct," said the editor.

"My favorite topic," B said with a wink.

There was a giant, glowing CK set up in front of a window overlooking the river. We walked through a selfie room, where classic Calvin Klein Underwear ads were projected onto a wall. I'd heard rumors that the *Times* was working on a story about Bruce Weber, who had taken many of these iconic photos. It was still early, but B wanted to leave.

"Two stops," he told the driver.

I asked B why. He said that he was tired and had to work in the morning. I was drunk and mad about a lot of things in my life. I hated my job and all the other guys I'd been going on dates with, and I wasn't over my recent breakup. It was clear that B had started dating someone. That he'd used me to get into the party, flirted with my friends, flaunted his connection to me, and always planned on meeting up with someone else later. Maybe he was planning on bringing her back to the pier. Did he want her to see that same scene, but with him as the protagonist?

My voice was rising, and B was gesturing with his hands that I needed to lower it. So I got louder and told him to get out at the next light. I didn't really mean it when I said I didn't want to speak to him again, but that's what ended up happening. Later I found out he was twenty-one—ten years younger than me.

November 7, 2017

China Chalet for an art auction. A friend, C, had just found out that her boyfriend, the director of a gallery, was cheating on her. C's editor was also at China Chalet. He'd brought along D, an intern from their magazine. The editor left, but D stuck around and joined us at a table.

"I can't look at Facebook anymore," D announced. "I'm too triggered by all this 'me too' stuff. I just don't want to read every single person's trauma story right now."

I'd read a good op-ed in the *Times* by Lupita Nyong'o, I said, about the way professional and personal boundaries were often blurred in filmmaking. "Our business is complicated because intimacy is part and parcel of our profession; as actors we are paid to do very intimate things in public," Nyong'o wrote. She demonized the perpetrators while tearing a little hole in the sheet that separated the people in power from their victims. This was why these cases fascinated me. It was like learning we were all part of a cult. Maybe there was a way out. But maybe there wasn't.

"Isn't Lupita Nyong'o transphobic?" D asked. The lights came on.

Outside the party, I saw E, a man I'd slept with once, years ago. C and I got into a cab, and D followed us inside. "Am I overstepping?" he asked.

"No, of course not," C said. We told the driver to take us to Clandestino.

C had noticed the weird moment between E and me on the sidewalk. "You know him, don't you?" she asked.

Around when I'd first moved to New York, I said, I'd gone home with E after a party and was so drunk I'd almost passed out in the car. We had sex on a sandy mattress on the floor of what counted as a room in his curtained-off loft, and I blacked out. I walked home in the morning thinking I'd never see him again, since he was a messy punk who lived with like ten roommates. But at a gallery opening a few weeks later, a friend introduced me to E as an old classmate from a prestigious art school. I smiled and said "Nice to meet you" and shook E's hand before I recognized him. He looked hurt and confused, and I turned bright red. But shouldn't I be the one who's upset? I said in the cab. He shouldn't have taken me home in that state.

"Yeah," C said. "I mean, *me too*."

"But who hasn't been in that situation?" D asked.

At Clandestino all the bar stools and tables were taken, so we each got a cocktail and stood in a circle. We started talking about skincare treatments. C and I were the same age and terrified of every line or acne scar we spotted while washing the mud masks off our faces every hungover Sunday. D said he wanted an alternative hair removal treatment because lasers wouldn't be able to detect his blond follicles.

"What hair do you want removed?" asked C.

"All of it except my head hair," he said, eyes wide and suddenly very serious. "I identify as hairless. But the treatment is really expensive," he added mournfully.

"You identify as hairless?" I asked.

"I don't necessarily want a constructed vagina," he said, clarifying. "I just want this hair removal procedure."

This felt like a non-sequitur, and it took me a few minutes to understand what D was saying: hairlessness would free him from the constraints of his cisgendered condition. It wasn't until the next day that I made the connection—his connection—between hairlessness and femininity. Did I also identify as hairless, or was it simply expected of me?

November 8, 2017

Some friends and I stood in line for champagne at an after-party for an arts gala at Halston's old townhouse. A famous young artist kissed both my cheeks. "Did you know that the guy who used to live here, he was this guy who hung out with Andy Warhol?"

A blond socialite wearing a high fake ponytail and Ray-Bans told me she liked my look. She wore a new Gucci dress with a sequined cape, and I had on the three-seasons-old JW Anderson sweater I'd worn to work that day over a wool skirt and black tights. She talked to me about what New York used to be, when she was out getting into trouble. She looked about my age. I learned that she'd been married once and engaged again, but the recent fiancé had gotten "heavy into drugs" and was now in rehab.

"That was all back in Malibu, you remember," she started saying to a friend, a giant man I recognized from last week's Halloween party at PS1. She introduced him to me as F. He didn't seem to recognize me. On Halloween, F had fed me bump after bump of coke from the wing of his hand in line for the bathroom and then asked me to come into a stall with him. His girlfriend was waiting downstairs, he said. In the stall we played a game of truth or dare. I'd picked dare.

"I dare you to show me any body part I want to see," F said, preparing another small pile. I hesitated, and he quickly said "Tits." I was wearing a sexy costume and felt like a different person, like I was in New York before it sucked, which is how I always felt at big parties full of drag queens and drugs. I pulled down my top for a half second.

"Truth or dare," I said. F picked dare.

"I dare you to give me more drugs," I said. F asked me to make out with him, and I left the stall. The friend I was with, a girl from another magazine, said we should go with F to the Boom Boom Room. "Something bad happened in there," I said, pointing to the bathroom.

"Yeah," she said, "before you got in line, I made out with him. He's a big art dealer, or curator, I forget."

At the Halston house, F was telling me about his wife and about old New York, spitting in my face with every sentence. I hated him, he was so ugly and uncool, and yet I didn't tell him he was spitting on me, or that he had called his wife his "girlfriend" when we'd met before, or that we'd met before. Then he started telling the socialite about the party on Halloween: "I was at the museum, and then I ended up at a warehouse party in god knows where, I really have no idea, and then at about six in the morning, I press a button and I'm in a car on my way home. Still have no clue where I was or what way the car took me to get back, but that's the future, isn't it? We're living in the future. I'm telling you, I'm having the best time I've ever had in New York. It's only getting better here."

Even the socialite looked confused by this. "Now?" she asked, frowning.

We were supposed to meet Rose McGowan at Café d'Alsace after the party, but she cancelled at the last minute. I saw on Twitter that she had been hit with a drug possession charge, which she insisted was a scheme to keep her Weinstein dirt quiet. I hadn't even read her Weinstein story. I'd read Asia Argento's, Gwyneth Paltrow's, and Lupita Nyong'o's, and then I'd stopped. The stories were so familiar and dark, but also loaded—I wanted to ignore their details. It was an instinctual reaction.

I still wanted to know that the articles were being published, and in large quantities, but reading stories of abuse and humiliation, like the big Bill Cosby exposé from a few years back, was as stupefying as a hangover. I didn't feel empowered; I only felt more hopeless. I wanted to watch the patriarchy go up in flames, but I wasn't excited about what was being pitched to replace it. If we got all of it out in the open, what would we have left? My fear was that guilt would destroy the classics and there'd be no one left to fuck. All movies would be as low-budget and puritanical as the stuff they play on Lifetime, all of New York would look like a Target ad, every book or article would be a cathartic tell-all, and I'd be sexually frustrated but too ashamed to hook up with assholes, or even to watch porn.

November 9, 2017

I left work early and went to my intake session at the city counseling center. I told an old woman very briefly about my family and my childhood and the man who broke my heart in grad school by cheating on me and the man who scandalized me just months ago by cheating on me with a lot of women in our shared field. I was happy with my career, I said. That was one thing I had under control. I'd initially wanted to go to therapy because I had writer's block. Now there were so many other reasons. My eyes clouded over, but I didn't let any tears fall. I wanted to seem strong, so I would be assigned a good, smart therapist.

The *Times* was keeping a running list of men who experienced professional fallout following accusations of sexual misconduct. Along the edge of the list were photos of guys with pale, drooping jowls, rosacea, male pattern baldness, glasses, bulbous noses, squat or too-narrow heads, and puffy bags under beady eyes set too close together.

I wasn't immune to finding power sexy. I'd gone out with men because I was impressed by their jobs, thought about leaving men and then remembered their jobs. I told myself that this wasn't a shallow train of thought, it was actually a tribute to a man's character: the position he held said something about him, something I was supposed to like. But now it was clear that the jobs, especially the impressive ones, were the parts I hated most about the men. The cheating happened at the office. Maybe it stemmed from the atmosphere there.

Later, I went to a performance that combined opera, modern dance, pornographic sex, and a stage play about modern technology and its effect on relationships. Afterward, a group of us took the train into Manhattan and tried several Lower East Side bars until we found a bearable one. I tried to tell a story about the extreme behavior of certain young millennials, but either it came out wrong or there was no right way to tell it. "He identified as hairless," I said. No one said anything in response.

We went to the park so some of us could smoke a joint, but it was cold out, and there were too many rats scurrying around. I shared a ride home with a comedian who had been very serious the entire night. In the cab she told me a story about a man she'd been seeing while she lived in Amsterdam. He was the lead singer in a band, and now a lot of the women he'd slept with on tour were speaking out about him possibly date-raping them after shows. She was still in love with him, but she didn't seem emotional or bitter at all.

"I tend to believe the victims," she said quietly. "It takes a lot of bravery to say something like that. People always say that victims come out of the woodwork to get attention, but really, how many women want that kind of attention? They're still interested in dating men, right? And they're going to have a much harder time doing that once they're known for calling out a rock star for misbehaving—oh, right here is fine," she told the driver.

November 10, 2017

I went to the gym and started sobbing on the treadmill. I texted my ex. I told him he had ruined my life and that I was so depressed I couldn't function. I told him I was crying at the gym, thinking this would provide him with a clarifying mental image. I thought about texting him other things, like how earlier that day I'd seen the neighbor's cat we used to play with together on my fire escape. The cat would come inside through the bathroom window and let us brush him. Alone that afternoon, I ran a comb through his thick fur, picking up a mass of gray undercoat while he purred. After a few minutes, he crawled back out the window, down the fire escape, and into my downstairs neighbor's bathroom window, where another cat who looked exactly like him was waiting. They hissed at each other and then both stepped inside. I wanted to tell my ex that it might have been two cats the whole time. Instead I texted him that he was a monster. He apologized again, and said that apologizing was all he could do.

November 11, 2017

I went to see some friends do stand-up. I laughed a lot, and then got anxious thinking about what I could contribute to this crowd. I wasn't funny at all. I hardly talked after the show, but my friends kept making sure I was involved in the conversation by bringing up things they knew about me. The whole experience made me emotional, which made me get even quieter. The bar closed, so we went to another bar. Someone did lines off a table. At one point everyone was in agreement about Kevin Spacey—it was totally normal, they said, to hit on a minor in your twenties.

"Gay teens have sex with old men," someone said. "There's a movie out about it right now. It's getting Oscar buzz!"

November 12, 2017

I stayed in my bedroom all day. When it got dark out I turned on the lights and went to the gym. At nine I went to a dinner party that honored the winner of an annual fashion fund. Everyone was happy and telling one another how happy they were. This was the most deserving recipient in the history of the award, we all said. An older man with one pearl earring walked in, and my friend and I talked about how great he looked.

Later on, he grabbed our asses at the same time and whispered into the space between our heads, "I'm not here. I have no name."

Another friend I hadn't seen in a while asked me about my boyfriend, and I had to tell him we'd broken up. Usually, people change the subject when I tell them, but he said, "He seemed like such a nice guy," so I had to fake a laugh and say, "Well, turns out he wasn't." After the ceremony, I put my headphones in and walked alone to West 4th.

The long, sloping passageway that led to the platforms was covered in ads for a grocery delivery app. Special Instructions: No Dressing, one said. It showed a cartoon man sitting on his couch, wearing only boxers. What do you know? Salmon does travel uptown, said another. On the lower train platform, another set of ads, this one for a phone with an improved selfie camera: Does Loving Yourself Have A Limit? The train charged in, blocking images of a duck-lipped woman in deep focus. I sat on an empty bench and looked up. Along the seams of the subway car's ceiling, a set of ads for a bedding company said, Get Dressed Never, 500 More Minutes, and Let's Not Run Away Together. I turned to read the vertical ad mounted behind me for an apartment listing app. Search: Separate Entrance for Roommate. There was a poster-sized ad further down on the train for something medical. The only part of a Spanish phrase I could translate was You Are Not Alone.

November 13, 2017

I got up and read the news of another public figure being accused of sexual harassment, like I did every day. At work, I went to a bathroom stall to either cry or get lost in a sexual fantasy about a man I was messaging via Tinder, or both, at different times. The days were getting shorter and darker and everyone was talking about bleakness and cuffing.

November 14, 2017

I met G at her apartment after work so we could go to a techno show we'd bought tickets to weeks earlier. She poured us two huge glasses of white wine. In the Lyft, I realized she was very drunk. We got to the venue in Gowanus and she stumbled out of the car. She stayed for a few minutes and tried to pull herself together, but ended up leaving before eleven. I stayed there, dancing alone.

The DJ I liked finally went on at one in the morning. I was very drunk. I felt hands on my thighs and turned around to face a girl with long blond hair, a lacy cleavage-baring bodysuit, and tight black jeans. She danced with me for a while and then danced with a girl with long black hair and a mesh top over a black bra. Then she came back to me and got closer and closer until we kissed. She yelled into my ear that the girl with black hair was her girlfriend, and then took my hand and led me to the back of the dance floor. We danced in circles and made out for what felt like hours. She had perfect teeth when she smiled. Eventually, she asked me how old I was, and I lied and said thirty. I should have said twenty-nine. Thirty is just as bad as thirty-one. She laughed and said she was twenty-two. She kissed me again to show me she didn't mind. She asked me where I lived, but the music was too loud for us to understand each other anymore, and she said she didn't know English well. When the girlfriend found us, the blonde started talking to her quickly in Spanish and laughing. They both laughed. I went to the bathroom and was glad to see that they were not in the same spot when I came out. It was almost three. I got in a cab that took me in a huge loop before the driver realized his mistake and then blamed it on me. I didn't argue.

November 15, 2017

The stories about Louis CK came out and I was devastated. The way he wrote about sex felt necessary to me. There were perverts everywhere, and we should understand them because we should understand the world we live in. It was easy to imagine that Louis thought what he was doing was attractive to the women he assaulted, even if it was traumatizing: when he did it on TV, people loved it. His new movie was cancelled, and everyone insinuated that he was a sicko who deserved to never work again. Maybe they were right, I don't know. But I wasn't ready to live in a world that censored a pervert honest enough to say he was perverted. It was his fault—he shouldn't have done those things. It was my fault, too. Maybe I shouldn't have loved his comedy. I shouldn't have shown that art dealer my tits on Halloween. Sometimes I felt guilty about loving the recklessness that came with being a woman.

Most days, I felt exhilarated when I read about men getting fired. I thought about my ex-boyfriend, who had cheated on me with women who were trying to advance their careers. This was an imbalance that was being abused. But he disagreed with me that his behavior was inappropriate, beyond the fact of his cheating. And yet I didn't want to start a campaign against him. I was afraid of looking petty, or worse, like a victim. I'd rather erase the memory, not explode it. Because if I hadn't been cheated on, I would have gone on thinking that I never could have been, which would have been preferable. Maybe if I didn't know about any of it, I'd be able to read about other women being humiliated.

Every time I broke up with someone, I'd go back to the gym. It was a different gym each time, because new gyms kept opening closer and closer to my apartment. My roommate, H, went to many gyms, too, but with greater consistency. His body was dense and angular; he drank protein shakes and carb loads or whatever, whereas I spent my time stretching and hunching in the mirror, trying to see more concave areas, more negative space between hips and ribs. No matter what, my weight read the same on the scale. I looked thinner and felt lighter, but the numbers didn't get smaller. I wanted to take up so little space that my coworkers would look at my chair, assess the amount of room left on either side of me, and not be able to mask their envy.

It was easier for me to give up eating than it was for me to give up drinking. I didn't stop eating, though, because then I'd have to stop going to the gym, and then I'd start smoking again.

November 16, 2017

After work I attended the simultaneous launches of a new smartphone and a new R&B album. The launches concluded with a pink neon-lit party, during which my friends and I took pictures of our new free phones with our old ones, drank free cocktails, and ate hors d'oeuvres you had to work for: From a back door came a procession of wooden planks strapped to smiling waiters that held anise-spiked dark chocolate that had to be chiseled off a bar, bunches of baby bananas in thick peels, persimmons with stems attached, skewers of shell-on shrimp, and white radishes that looked like they'd just been pulled from a field. G said she was keeping her old phone and her new one: one for personal use and one for sponsored posting. "It has a really good camera," she said.

Later, I met up with a brand consultant for a second date. I started telling him about other Tinder dates I'd been on. I lied and said that they'd all happened before our first date, which was weeks ago. I kept doing this, for some reason: comparing everyone I'd just met to everyone else I'd just met, aloud, to their faces. Guys lied about their ages lot, I said. A forty-year-old said he was thirty-six, and a forty-eight-year-old said he was forty-four. Should I be lying about my age? I wanted to attract people my age or older than me, I said. If I said I was in my twenties, I could start attracting twenty-somethings, whom I hated. Don't you? I asked.

He stared forward, blank faced. No thirty-something man hates twenty-somethings, he said. Was I anxious about aging? he asked.

The anxiety was what I was supposed to lie about. All thirty-something women are supposed to say they are excited to finally feel adult and to know themselves. But I didn't lie about that. I said if I was anxious about anything, it was becoming obsolete, in my career and in my sex life. He was surprisingly sympathetic. He wanted to have sex with me, though. I wanted to have sex with someone, so it may as well be him.

November 18, 2017

I went with C to the Women's Entrepreneurship Day fundraising pre-dinner. In the lobby, we told a woman with an iPad who we were, and another girl took us to a private elevator, whose operator knew what floor to take us to. When the doors opened, another attendant took our coats and gave us tickets. A short hallway opened to an apartment painted in bright colors and hung with paintings and artifacts of world travels. Two bichons wearing hot pink fleece vests and diamante-studded collars clinked around a tiered table full of champagne bottles. A man was filling flutes and placing them on a tray held by another man. Another man was ladling a creamy pink punch into short goblets and handing them to women wearing Chanel suits and costume jewelry.

The publicist who had invited us introduced us to the owner of the apartment, a woman whose face was asymmetrical with botched plastic surgeries. She was wearing a pink fleece vest, too, and furry pink slippers. Many of the attendees looked to be mothers in pearls with their daughters, who wore Tiffany charm bracelets or Cartier bangles. The publicist and the wait staff were the only men in the room, until a man walked in with his younger wife. Her Hervé Léger dress squeezed her upper back, giving it a long crease. It took the man only a few minutes to find a reason to talk to a famous model who was sipping a clear cocktail near the window. The trophy wife stood patiently to the side. The owner of the apartment, now holding a dog under each arm, posed in front of a small step-and-repeat that blocked a doorway. Someone handed her a microphone and took one of the dogs from her so she could hold it. She talked for a few minutes about her home, her dogs, and her career as a film producer.

The founder of Women's Entrepreneurship Day, a "leading activist," mentioned how close she was to each of the dogs, how much character they had, and how her own dog loved them like sisters. What followed was hard to follow. It was a winding speech about activism—first animal-rights activism, and then something vague about underprivileged women, a half-told anecdote about a stalker, something about writing several books and breaking several Guinness World Records, and then a story that started with, "No one told me that Honduras isn't a vacation spot." If it wasn't for her trip to Honduras—"Which I do not recommend, by the way; it's the most dangerous place in the world, did you guys know this? I didn't"—she would have never met so many women in need of business training. And that was the goal for the fundraiser the following night, to which everyone was required to bring their checkbooks.

November 19, 2017

At some point on Sunday, in bed, I Googled the owner of the apartment. Her one film credit was a short she'd written, directed, produced, and voiced. It starred her two dogs. Next I Googled the speaker. Her books were mostly about her dogs, and her Guinness World Records were for dog with the most expensive wedding and dog photographed with the most celebrities. I texted C about it.

"If I see her on the street I will throw something at her," she replied.

November 20, 2017

I swiped through Tinder at work and went on a date with someone I'd matched with hours earlier, J. He looked like an older Ryan Gosling.

"It's weird, because that guy isn't that attractive, right? But because he's so charming, he is. And now I am, by association."

After one drink, he insisted we talk about the abuse allegations against Al Franken, Louis CK, and Lars von Trier. Everyone I went out with brought up sexual harassment, which made me uneasy. They all spoke with the same, flippant tone about women getting ahead of themselves or making bigger deals about certain things than was productive. It was as if they were making sure I wasn't one of the ones who would get hysterical. At least J backtracked a little and then let me change the subject. We'd both just seen *The Square* and liked it, and he'd just broken up with someone, too, and thirty-one seemed so young to him. We went from a bar in Ridgewood to a club in Greenpoint and danced to minimal techno until two. An obscure song started playing and we both said, "I love this song" at the same time. At the end of our date, he put me in a cab and kissed me and said, "We should stay in touch."

November 21, 2017

A growing percentage of my texts were from men who wanted to "stay in touch." We had inside jokes, we sent one another articles about things we'd discussed on our dates, we even started telling one another about other dates we'd been on, commiserating about what the app was doing to our minds.

There were many men, most of whom I'd met and at least made out with: a lawyer, a garbage man, a magazine editor, a TV camera operator, a CEO, a graphic designer, a social media analyst, a photojournalist, a married woman who had no job. I didn't quite feel rejected by any of them. It was about chemistry, I told myself. Some seemed intimidated by my busy life. Others were hung up on an ex and just wanted to hook up, but found that texting me later was fun, too. I knew that J wasn't going to want to date me, which only hurt because he was perfect on paper. His detached kiss and all the conversations tapering off into platonic feelings made me sad, and I started to cry, as I often did lately, without warning. Was I not irresistible to anyone? Was being irresistible to men what I wanted the most, out of anything in the world?

November 22, 2017

I was emailing a man from my past, a new divorcé. "Stop that," said H. I switched to the conversations on Tinder with guys who were old enough to be my father. There were messages I left unanswered, some about sex and others about expensive dates and still others about the full moon that night or the delicious meal they made from scratch, alone. Sometimes they would enter my fantasies, their hunger more interesting than the other, brutish kind of lust.

These men were happy to repeatedly ask for my attention, and maybe even happy that our dynamic meant that I often acted callous toward them. I wanted them to continue to want me, but I couldn't imagine becoming exclusive with someone so fascinated by my autonomy. I sent a series of texts to a man in his late forties I'd been on one boring date with. He was away on a business trip in an earlier time zone. "Hello, darling," he wrote back, as if we were in a full-blown relationship. That kind of thing didn't used to bother me so much.

November 23, 2017

H and I went to a Thanksgiving party at our friend's West Village apartment. We brought a green bean casserole and a ham. I was surprised to see an acquaintance of my ex, and more surprised to find out that he hadn't heard we'd broken up. "But you guys had some kind of understanding, right? You weren't, like committed."

I couldn't help myself. "He wasn't," I said. "I was."

"I never knew, by the way, that you're a writer. Why didn't you tell me?"

"I assumed he would have told you that," I said, stunned again.

"You can never expect anyone to do your promotion," he said. "I learned that the hard way." I knew that he wanted me to ask about his own writing career, but I didn't.

I excused myself to get a glass of wine. A woman I didn't know well sat by me during the dinner. She said she'd gotten back together with her ex, who had broken off their engagement a year earlier. C was there with her boyfriend, the gallerist. They'd gotten back together, too. After dinner, H, C, and I went to the Thursday night strip club in the basement of the Monster. I had never seen male strippers before. As a woman, I wasn't allowed to get a lap dance, which meant none of the men walking by us would paw my shoulder or kiss my cheeks. They just smiled and winked. "A lot of them are straight," said H. "Like, a lot."

Some could pole dance almost as well as female strippers, and others simply stood on the stage and flexed. There wasn't a correlation I could trace between skill and tips, only one between attractiveness and tips. C got a phone call from her boyfriend and had to leave. I could see tears forming in her eyes when she hugged us to say goodbye. H disappeared into the lap dance room. I was alone, a handful of ones ready to fold into a waistband if I was impressed enough by a silently dancing man. It was still Thanksgiving, and the MC hadn't mentioned the holiday once. I was surrounded by older men, but it was like they didn't see me. If I didn't know why, I'd be sad about that, but since I did know why, I was happier than I'd been in months.

Consulting

Just before things started heating up in the 2016 presidential campaign, I quit my job at a fashion magazine. I'd been working there for four years, almost the entire time I'd lived in New York. I just couldn't take it anymore—the meetings, the late nights, the peripheral view of chic parties. The perks had started to feel more like obligations.

Meanwhile, I'd gotten a temp job as a copywriter for an app. The team met in an office in Midtown, one of a few operated by a company called IFGM Ltd. This office was mostly used for one of IFGM's other media businesses, a news site known for its proprietary deep web analysis called SearchInfo.

Dominic was another ex-editor from the magazine I'd just left. He and I had both been hired as "consultants" here. Dom would do most of the talking at the office. We were not developers or designers. Neither of us could even present our ideas clearly to the CEOs, with whom we were regularly in meetings at long tables covered in fruit and cheese. We'd never even made PowerPoint presentations. We were hired because we knew about media and where it was going, apparently, having had worked in media.

The office manager here, Yael, wanted us temps to develop an app that used facial recognition to do something. So far, we already had the subscribers of a once popular fashion and lifestyle app—we were taking it over, or "re-launching" it. The facial recognition technology was still being baked into the backend. This new version of the old app would use deep web analysis, like SearchInfo did, but we wouldn't be gathering statistics for news reporting. We were going to sell information about the user and the user's Facebook friends to other companies. Subscribers of the existing app would be sent new terms of agreement and this would all be explained there.

The company who originally owned the fashion and lifestyle app had fired the developers when they thought developers were no longer needed to maintain it. There were glitches and the subscription rate plateaued, so they sold it to IFGM. Now, I was told, we had to do something with facial recognition in order to get the app to consistently gather information from subscribers. Social media and dating had all the advertising opportunities because of geo-tagging and cameras, Yael said.

Dom and I knew about fashion, which is linked to the beauty industry. But really we knew nothing about new media or beauty. Those areas, like web development, were lucrative, with endless possibilities and high stakes. No, we couldn't tell you about anything about that (although Dom would probably tell you that he could). We only knew about the antiquated print world that we'd once coveted, in part because it looked like it was slipping away.

Magazines needed saving, but no one could possibly save them, so no one would blame us if we failed trying. It wasn't heroic, jumping onto a sinking ship just to say we'd at least been on one, but we'd always loved magazines and it was the last chance anyone had to be a part of them. Now, our print magazine had all but sunk, and yet we were brought on to jump-start this muddily defined new digital platform—to re-launch something we never would have been able to create in the first place.

It needed to be about beauty, our new boss said. That was the obvious answer. It needed to have an excuse to take your picture, a selfie. It needed you to want to take selfies through the app instead of through any other app or through your regular camera. I did not pretend to know why that part was necessary.

On my last day at the magazine, a Friday, the art director there superimposed my face onto a cover featuring Selena Gomez and printed it out on cardstock. Everyone signed the back and we went out for drinks at Forlini's. And that was it, my dream job over. The following Monday, I went to the IFGM office. Dom had already been there for a month. He'd been given the desk of someone who was working remotely for the summer. It was a laminate table in a horrible little room with one office chair and a gray loveseat that was a far cry from the Eames chairs we'd had at the magazine. I was to share the room with him and bring my own computer. If we opened the fifth-floor window, we could hear sirens and honking as loud as if we were on the street. There were no potted orchids or skylights with automated screens that rolled over them when it was too sunny. The receptionist never learned my name.

There was something comforting about the anonymity, though. Here, people didn't ask what I was getting for lunch and then roll their eyes when I'd list the unhealthy buffet restaurants in my price range. The pantry was always stocked with Oreos, M&Ms, and Ritz crackers. Every day, I would bring my laptop out of a tote bag that said the name of the magazine I used to edit and lay down with my legs over one arm of that cheap loveseat. It was actually a really nice way to work. Dom and I would shut the door and stare at our screens while we gossiped about ex-coworkers and editors at other magazines, pretending to be busy so no one bothered us.

After my first week of work, I met up with my friend Elle at Fanelli. I told her how awful Midtown was and that I hadn't made any new friends at IFGM. "If you hate it, you should quit right away," said Elle. "Didn't you learn that from your last job?" Elle didn't have a job. I wanted to say that I'd learned a lot from my last job, but not that. It was hard to explain, though, since I'd complained incessantly about the magazine to her.

"I guess I should quit," I said. Why had I suggested this place? I was getting paid enough now to go to a nicer bar. I'd ordered a martini, which wasn't quite cold or dirty enough. Of course I should quit before the three months were up, but not because I disliked the location or the people. I could hide in that room for hours and sometimes I would leave before six. I only hated this job as much as I hated any job. I should have quit, though, because it was this bigger thing, this thing I couldn't even bear to think about.

IFGM was founded and owned by a man who spent most of his time in Israel, and there were rumors he was a major arms dealer there. The company had other New York offices that sold security software, which seemed strange since the one I worked for banked on gathering information from security loopholes.

"You're overqualified," Elle said. So many people in New York didn't have jobs now and never had. The rich ones were always pretending to be looking for the perfect job. They were overqualified for everything. I could work at a lot of places, but nowhere was I "qualified." Besides, everyone younger than me had a degree in marketing or branding or merchandising or content management or data analysis or coding. Even musicians had some sort of tech degree. I was becoming one of those people I couldn't stand, the people who had seen another time and couldn't stop talking about how great it was then because no one had needed a second college degree to be successful. But people my age could never genuinely complain they'd seen a better New York, since our New York is kind of like any other city but more expensive. Those who grew up here and those who lived here in the eighties could say what *was* New York, but they hardly talked about what *is* New York. New York is an actor, playing itself. We like to talk about the restaurants where everyone goes and the popular parties, but only because it is so New York to do so.

"My office is connected to four other companies," I said to Elle. "Basically all the major media agencies are right there. I'm not burning any of those bridges." I'd been in meetings with people who had handed me their cards afterward, who were described as "a really good person to know." It was as if Dom and I were doing something that people really wanted to be involved with, and with which people wanted to involve their huge clients. The app we were working on was partially owned by a huge media agency and a huge modeling agency and a huge tech company, I was told. I was also told, later, that none of this was true.

If you Googled the founder of IFGM, you'd find WikiLeaks articles and a video of him talking with Bill Clinton about the issue of cyber security. Conspiracy bloggers had described him as "evil." I hadn't even thought to Google him until he was in the office one day and some coworkers whispered that I should smile and say hello when I saw him instead of looking down and shuffling into my room. He liked when his employees smiled, they said. His suit looked expensive next to all the IT guys. Dom hadn't come in that day, so I was alone in our room, sitting at the desk with the door open. It was close to six and I was getting ready to leave when the founder walked in and sat on the gray loveseat. He asked me what my name was and what I was doing there.

"I'm consulting," I said.

"What is it that you *do*, though?"

"I'm a writer," I responded. I felt like I'd told him what I wanted to be when I grew up.

"Do you live in the city?" he asked.

"Brooklyn."

He said he owned a few apartments in Manhattan but felt lonely in them, so he always stayed at the Plaza. "When I come to New York, I call, and they reserve my room; they put the kind of furniture I like in it, because I don't like the regular furniture they have there."

I'd worked a photo shoot at the Plaza once and couldn't imagine moving that old-fashioned furniture out of those ornate rooms. If he hated the furniture and his own apartments, why didn't he stay at another one of the many hotels overlooking Central Park? Even though he was telling me where he was staying that night, I didn't feel like he was hitting on me. It was more like he was running on autopilot after a long day, maybe warming up for the Plaza bar.

I'd only stayed this late because there were meetings all day and I didn't know what to do other than go to them. In the meetings, though, I said nothing, scribbling certain words people would say aloud in my notebook. None of it meant anything to me, but I was fascinated. How does one learn to speak business? All of these people had normal, almost stupid conversations with each other in the mornings about mundane things, and then they would switch gears and eliminate all extra sounds, no ums or likes. They would talk about maximizing and optimizing and leveling engagement. And then I'd get asked a question, usually about a celebrity, something like, "Is she cool?" And I'd say, "Um, cool? Depends on, like, your audience."

It was dark out when the founder left. I sat at the table and for the first time really tried to think of ideas that would work for this project. The deadline was fast approaching and we had nothing. Maybe I'd stay late with the graphic designers and make some headway. Beauty. Facial recognition. There had to be something there. The app could recognize beauty. It could recommend to a user who wasn't beautiful all the ways to become beautiful. That wouldn't work, though, because it had to recommend ways to become beautiful to someone forever. After a while, a user would stop trusting an app that always said she wasn't pretty, right?

"Makeup is the bread and butter of fashion labels," I'd always heard from the magazine's publisher. Beauty advertising would have saved us, maybe. But who wants to write about that? Beauty editors are supposed to let you know what products are worth getting, and, paradoxically, they always have to tell you to buy something new. Editors are actually the women who have tried everything and stick to Vaseline around the eyes and coconut oil on the hair. They don't wear anything new, ever. They tan in the Hamptons and get manicures from one trusted salon. All of their body hair is gone, so they don't have to keep looking for ways to get rid of it.

What could our app do that other apps with facial recognition did not? I was the wrong person for this job. I didn't use FaceTune, FaceApp, FaceSwap, or even FaceTime. What I didn't like about all of them was that you have to look at yourself. The idea of prepping for selfies still made me feel sick and hopeless. I'd never be as beautiful as I used to be, back before smartphones existed. Every time I looked at my feed, I'd invariably see a girl with Jessica Rabbit-like proportions post a video of herself dancing, over a caption about her battles with "confidence." I scribbled down a few notes about body dysmorphia but came up with nothing related to branding or new tech. I wanted a cigarette and didn't want to come back inside once I was finished, so I left the half-full office to walk through Times Square and take two air-conditioned trains home.

Eventually, we decided on a technology that measured one's "mood" via selfie. Everyone at the office tested it and we were always told we were "blue." It was my job to copyedit the language around the moods. Dom had quit in a fiery tantrum by then. It was pretty similar to the way he'd quit the magazine. The new rumor about Dom was that he had a drug problem. I was almost positive he didn't. I was mad at him, but then again I was always mad at him until I realized he'd seen something before I could.

When the re-launch went live, it alerted its subscribers of its new functions. "Take a mood selfie," the app instructed. The mood was supposed to become a filter for content, eventually, but the developers hadn't quite worked that part out yet. The question remained: If one was "blue," would one want to see "blue" content, or content that would cheer them up? All the graphics were stock images of smiling women in black and white with a color gradient overlay based on the mood. Blues for "blue" and purples for "excited," etc. For the press release, I couldn't write that the mood function did anything, since it didn't. We were also carefully avoiding invasive language. I couldn't use the words "tailored" or "algorithm." Instead, we pushed that the app would have lots of prize giveaways and live Q&As using a forum similar to Reddit's, without mentioning Reddit.

I was hired to stay on for at least another month after the launch. I'd written the press releases about the app's functions, but each was heavily edited by someone in another office and then sent without my sign off. I was worried that so far I'd been pretty useless. Yael talked to me in the kitchen about this, saying I needed to believe in my self-worth. Everyone there was there because we were supposed to be. Sometimes, the best thing someone can contribute is good energy. "Okay," I said.

I tweeted that the books on Yael's shelf were called *Good to Great, Great by Choice, Make Winning a Habit, Bold, Hope is not a Strategy*, and *Daring Greatly*. I was pretty sure she'd be voting for Trump. If you Googled Yael, who was also from Israel, you'd just get a few pictures of her with the IFGM founder at events in New York. She would probably be very pretty if she didn't sleep at her desk so often. She was a shoe-addict, she told me when I caught her shopping online for more Jimmy Choos. She was always taking her heels off. "Pain is beauty," she'd say.

I was just getting into watching *The Real Housewives of New York City*. I'd avoided it until I found out that these women were all somehow connected to or vocally impressed by the Trump family, and then it felt too relevant to ignore. The show started out as a cloudy little window into a ridiculous world. But then I got caught up and it was sometimes tough to stay on the right side of the fence. The show was so good at pitting you against one in order to side with another. Just as Trump was making headway in his campaign, it was getting more difficult for me to come away from an old episode saying that absolutely no one on the show was in the right and that their values were all fucked up.

There was no moral compass. Someone said that all literature either began with a man going on a journey or a stranger coming to town but neither was happening here. Everyone was already in New York. And if you asked them, they ran New York. And since they were all involved in real estate, there was no reason to not believe it.

About a year before I quit the magazine, Dom and I came up with a story that enlisted artists to interpret one of the biggest events of 2015. We thought it was a no-brainer that someone would do Trump's ludicrous announcement about running for office. Artists painted Caitlyn Jenner's *Vanity Fair* cover and sculpted Rhonda Rousey winning a title and photographed a rainbow that could symbolize legal gay marriage in some states. No artist agreed to choose Trump as a subject, though. Either they knew his political career was destined to be more than simply an event in 2015, or, more likely, they thought that it wasn't even that.

Reality TV, like political campaigning, is all form, all narrative devices. We're tricked and then tricked again until the only redeemable character is the one everyone started out hating. Dishonesty becomes a scale. Desperation becomes endearing. Plastic surgery melds with natural features. What at first alarms a person becomes a sign of resilience. We call it the uncanny valley, or the physical incarnation of insecurity, these frozen facial expressions. Then we say that someone with visible scarring looks fabulous "for her age." Or better: She looks like she does not have an age.

New York felt very anti-Trump and yet it *was* Trump. This city made Trump, and friends of his were all around us. Similarly, it didn't always register that the real housewives of New York City lived where I did, and then I'd see a beautiful apartment building and wonder: if my life got swapped with one of theirs, would I act any differently? Was marrying rich the only way for some women to become rich? I wasn't supposed to think of Trump as a physical thing—as ugly and fat and old—but it was another of many contradictions brought up with his candidacy. If he was so rich, why did he look so bad? If I were in the public eye, would I get plastic surgery? What did he, or any of these reality stars, see in the mirror?

I was laid off from the temp job earlier than expected because the budget was somehow spent. I felt a little relieved to be leaving.

Then Trump was elected. It was shocking, and then it was outrageous, every day, and then it was soaked up by my surroundings until anything could be infuriating if presented the wrong way. I felt like I was always PMSing. In the so-called kleptocracy, it was exhausting trying to reiterate how insane everything felt in the beginning, and how normal it was starting to feel now. I received an email every day from an organization that suggested ways of fighting back. Almost every email was about calling a government official. I tried a couple times and left voicemails. Then I stopped. The emails piled up, telling me to join a chorus of complaints each morning before getting on the crowded J train into garbage-strewn Chinatown for my newest temp job, until one day I deleted all of them and unsubscribed. I didn't feel good about it.

Trump's tweets themselves were full of grammatical holes, which later worked in his favor, sort of. The scare quotes could mean anything he wanted them to. Inflammatory remarks could be part of a brilliant plan of distraction. But the graphic designs of the White House's internet presence gave away the lack of calculation behind the president's social media strategy. These tweeted images of group portraits reminded me of stressful conversations I'd had in meetings, on which I'd given up quickly.

Each Trump post was a gridded cluster of images that had been designed in Photoshop instead of dropped into the Twitter album function. They each used a different type, color, and weight of frame, with captions in a range of fonts embedded into photographs with drop shadows, haloed edges, or color blocks. Sometimes those captions had wildly incorrect punctuation.

The Trump Twitter profile banner was always being updated. Random example of one design: Under that image of the president surrounded by his employees, all of them raising their thumbs, was a black bar, and on it, white text that read, "Director Clapper reiterated what everybody, including the fake news media already knows- there is 'no evidence' of collusion w/ Russia and Trump." Next to this was a Twitter logo: that blue bird silhouette, only white.

I imagined a heated conversation between some White House officials and the press team's designers that probably sounded like what my old bosses would say to me about social media constraints: "I don't care what other people do; this is what *we* do!" They could never understand that breaking free of the restrictions—like a limited amount of characters in an official font, pictures that free-fall into a frameless slideshow, and Tweets that can only be pinned to the top of a feed, not above it—didn't work in the way it did for magazine layouts or billboards. Designing ads and articles, one was encouraged to think outside of boxes. But leaving the boundaries of Twitter, like this bizarrely placed quote did, literally took one out of the loop.

At the magazine or at IFGM I could always sway people in a conversation by using the phrase "out of touch." Another one was the idea of desperation. More important than gaining followers or views was avoiding looking desperate for followers or views.

Amidst many alleged terrorist attacks around the world and hearings about the Russians influencing the presidential election, attacks on the press felt less and less violent. But without the moral compass of the newspaper, we were all in some horrifying reality show about who was the most credulous at any given moment. People could shift from bad to good in the very next episode. If there was a stranger coming to town here, it was Trump himself. But he had been here the whole time.

I had still never seen the re-launched app. I was afraid to download it on my phone, knowing the amount of information it could mine from me. On some level, I knew that this was happening to me already because even when I wasn't on it, my phone's microphone was picking up conversations and feeding my locations to advertisers.

About six months after I was laid off, I read a headline: "'Fake news' site SearchInfo fires entire editorial staff and bulks up video team." The article joked that the site couldn't prove that its analysis technology was any more in-depth than their competitors. I was surprised that SearchInfo was in the press at all. They were a large staff who were always proudly projecting numbers, like "fourth-most shared stories on Facebook" (with highest numbers in Israel), but I had never heard of it before working for IFGM. The article noted that the SearchInfo/IFGM founder said in a statement that he had compensated every staffer with a severance package and that even more money would go into video production. He was clearly afraid that people would view the layoffs as a warning sign about his business. In fact, the news was good, he said. As I read it, I remembered what he said about the Plaza: a mogul like him could own Manhattan property and still choose to stay at what many considered the nicest hotel in New York, not that it was nice enough for him.

Also in the article, an ex-staffer called SearchInfo "an Israeli billionaire's vanity project," laughing off the notion that they were writing "fake news" in America. "We broke news about fake news," he said. This quote was linked to an InfoSearch article about Ukrainian teenagers writing about Hillary Clinton's concentration camps. The piece ended with a mention of the founder's next venture: a scripted TV series about hackers.

I sent a link to Dom, who I assumed would freak out. It was all turning out to be like the plot of a science fiction movie, in which everyone could be lying. I pictured all of our past bosses and the politicians who were supposedly friends with them and all the reporters on the news turning out to be automatons, their heads swiveling toward us, their faces already smudged in conflicting directions due to what we'd assumed was Botox. I imagined their skin finally melting off to reveal sparking circuit boards. Dom would know the answer to this one. He always knew the dark backstory of something before anyone else did. Dom's reply was about as informative as any email we'd received from any of these androids, though. "LOL," he wrote, "weird."

Press Release

The group of New York writers who look like nineties supermodels—laughing, wearing white pants to accentuate hips and flat stomachs—were having a cocktail they'd read about in a Vanity Fair article from the nineties and they were having more fun. More fun than the artists, was the point. It was a dinner for an art magazine, but that meant it was a dinner for the writers. Or at least they would make sure it felt that way for everyone else. The artists were mostly beautiful, too, but they were made to feel guilty about that sometimes, and so their chosen dress was somewhere between sexy and frumpy, disheveled Milan Kundera characters. It wasn't looking good for any of the women there with hopes of getting laid.

It wasn't looking good for the editor of the magazine, either: the girl he'd hired to write about the party for another publication was very drunk, and the meal had yet to be served. This hired writer leaned over the table to say hello to a woman whose art she thought she liked, but wasn't sure.

"I know your work," she said. "It's nice to meet you."

The artist was flattered. She wasn't well known, but a big collector had recently bought two of her pieces and her gallerist was more optimistic than ever. She knew who this writer was, and couldn't help but want to be her. The writer was thin and tall and black and friends with all the kids who admitted to being rich and who had parties in beautiful town houses.

"It's nice to meet you, too," said the artist, who was white and not tall. "I know your work as well." By work she meant popularity. She must be a good writer, though, to have gotten so much attention. Was the writer rich too? She was wearing a Tom Ford dress and gold bracelets, but anything could be borrowed or fake. As an artist, was she supposed to be able to tell, or was it better that she didn't know?

The collector had purchased her pieces from a Lower East Side group show. Every artist in it was female, but that wasn't the point of it. The next thing she did shouldn't be so body-centric, she thought, looking at all the other artworks. But when she sat in her studio, thinking about what to do next—the move after what would come to be viewed as her first one—her gaze would drift to the window. Through it, a Mylar balloon bobbed on a tree branch, its remaining opaque color confettied around a silver seam. It had likely been a pink balloon once, one that welcomed a baby girl into existence. How could she think outside of her body, she thought, again: the body, the outside world that defines my body, the body… and: my art is the only part of the outside world I can define. But the writer, what was she? It was settled that they would go home together. Neither wanted to back down from the other's silent dare to hook up with a woman for the first time; it was just a question of whose place. The studio, in Chinatown, was closer than both of their apartments.

Surrounded by her own lack of art, the artist kissed the writer. Each woman had the crippling thought at many points throughout their one-night stand that it would be fun for someone else to watch this. The writer left when it started getting light out and hated herself for not getting an angle on the party. She hadn't really looked at this artist's work when she was in front of it. She'd been too drunk and nervous.

"She's great," said her friend, another writer who'd been at the party and saw them leave together. "Just write the piece about your impromptu studio visit." Later that day, after a very short nap, the writer's recap became the first real press on the artist, describing her drawings as "not just boundary-breaking, but boundary re-establishing."

Maybe one day the artist would make portraits of the writer, in return for the writer's portrait of her. That's how it happened, said her friend. They helped each other out. The writer wrote her biggest article right after that, and so the party recap got spillover traffic from people trying to figure out who this brilliant woman was. The artist's next body of work was those sun-faded couches with the outlines of people on them. You know the ones. Those were great.

Internet as Horror

As part of the generation that defines stages of our lives as pre and post-something in terms of our evolving language (email, Instant Message, mobile, Google, social media), it's easy to imagine that the next shift in how we communicate will have a lot to do with the so-called post-truth era. Our awareness of native advertising, artificial intelligence, and data mining has impacted levels of trust in all forms of communication. In fact, digital and IRL subcultures are developing based on ideas around the nature of "truth" itself (see: Flat Earthers).

To better understand concepts that are unwieldy or intangible, we implement metaphors. As linguists George Lakoff and Mark Johnson argued in their seminal 1980 book *Metaphors We Live By*, "Our ordinary conceptual system, in terms of which we both think and act, is fundamentally metaphorical in nature." Examples support this notion, like "happy is up and sad is down." In other words, most concepts with positive connotations are metaphorically described with the up direction: "spirits rising," "high morale," "climbing the corporate ladder," while most negative concepts are metaphorically down: "feeling low," "down in the dumps," "sinking fast."

Linguistic metaphors are chosen above other ideas related to the same intangible concepts, perhaps almost arbitrarily. Happy could have been expansive, like a smile, for example, while sad could have been narrow. We stick to the rule of directional metaphor when it comes to most ideas of positivity and negativity, if only to simplify. But with every simplification of our language, new complexities emerge. Slang, abbreviations, and new uses for words develop with parallel trends. This is where metaphors in language are called to task: our understandings of them must withstand the elasticity and evolution of everyday communication.

Early metaphors used in conjunction with the internet were perhaps only consistent in their tangible treatment of it: We talked about the internet as water to be "surfed," with "torrents" and "streams," as a grid, "web," or "'net," marked with "sites," and as a building, with (chat) "rooms," (message) "boards," "walls" on which to "post," and "windows."

New uses for words are invented every year in terms of what we do on the internet, and no one metaphor seems to have become entirely pervasive so far, but lately, the vocabulary developed to describe new internet-only behaviors seems to fear the internet itself, likening it to a horror story in which users "troll," "ghost," and go "viral."

Modes of vocabulary change faster than the metaphors we use to describe concepts. We absorb the content that we can see and are influenced by its language. Naturally, while academic, political, and journalistic language has always set the tone for argument, the phrasing used in social media rants and comment sections has started to influence academia, politics, and journalism. And since language isn't a feedback loop, this inversion of influence has birthed new phrases and terms, evolving with demand for specificity.

In the study of linguistics, it is considered dangerous to assume too much about the way words affect a culture and normal to assume that a culture affects words. For example, we can assume that the newer definition of "viral" was created in response to the culture's disdain for said behavior, but assuming that the chosen word itself might influence the way we treat said behavior is a stretch: We can easily describe the spread of sensational content as virus-like, but that does not mean that we will next be researching a cure for viral media.

This is generally the trajectory of these types of linguistic trends. But with the rise of trolling (Google dictionary: "troll—verb 1. make a deliberately offensive or provocative online post with the aim of upsetting someone or eliciting an angry response from them") we have witnessed the rise of the ultimate trolls in power.

The president's language, heard in his speeches and seen on his Twitter account, is outrageous, yet all too familiar: it's also used by teenagers berating peers anonymously in comment sections, and by celebrity super fans defending their idols. The linguistics of online trolling has trickled down into the lexicon of real life, like in political campaigns and reportage.

The immediate validation model of online messaging has made applicable a new set of expectations. Additionally, the chance of a public encounter with a stranger encourages sensational behavior. Celebrities like Trump use emphatic language to reach the lowest common denominator—the rule of the simpler the message, the easier it is to agree with—in the same way protest chants and hashtags do. Celebrity-followers, on the other hand, use emphatic language in order to gain the most traction, as an effort to eventually reach the eyes of said celebrity. Both types of trolling have degraded to violent threats, personal attacks, and bigotry in the name of reach. If a topic proves controversial enough, after a wave of shaming comes a wave of defending, and so on, until the topic is trending.

If all visibility is good visibility, a tornado of trolling is the best possible scenario. Although no publicity firms have outright admitted it, it seems obvious that certain commercials are trolling themselves. A Heineken ad, for example, that came under fire for the plotline of a cold beer sliding past three African American people to land before an Asian woman, followed by the slogan "Sometimes, lighter is better," was pulled after a celebrity (Chance the Rapper) called it out.

"I think some companies are purposely putting out noticably [*sic*] racist ads so they can get more views. And that shit racist/bogus so I guess I shouldn't help by posting about it. But…I gotta just say tho. The 'sometimes lighter is better' Hienekin commercial is terribly racist omg," tweeted Chance. Now, when searching the slogan on YouTube, dozens of videos that play the full ad come up, including coverage by the news and late night talk shows, totaling millions of views.

With the naming of call-out culture—essentially, trolling the trolls—we've had no choice but to become confused about who tells the truth, since neither trolling or calling out are based in the principles of what we once gave credence: traditional journalism and academic research. This, what I'm writing, isn't either. It's a think piece, or an op ed, or a rant, depending on who you ask. Or maybe it's a work of fiction (have we any need for fiction now, when nothing can be proven to be nonfiction?).

We know that technology impacts our communication—the way we argue a point, how patient we are with response time—but we also know that the language we use in order to adapt to new technology must eventually impact our lives as well. The term "ghosting" was developed in parallel to the rise of near-constant communication. Before we were always essentially available to anyone with our information, a term to describe no longer responding to someone wasn't necessary. Now, ghosting is part of our dating culture, a key to understanding a typified relationship. The term feels necessarily specific, based on how dating has changed since the advents of so many messaging apps.

We remember a time before the terms "cyber-bullying" and "gas-lighting" affected our reactions to everyday occurrences, and a time before these reactions produced their own new phrases and philosophies. Streaming services have made it so "binge-watching" is a thing, as opposed to something less risky-sounding. We describe our "addictions" to new media in all seriousness, taking rehabilitating hiatuses from online availability. While a "safe space" isn't necessarily offline, it is easier to imagine that most are. The casual victimization derived from a world of socializing apps has perhaps created what we call a "fuckboy" and "rape culture." Trending terminology appears to only grow more violent and melodramatic on social media, with abbreviations like "kys" ("kill yourself") replacing the popular troll, "delete your account."

Studies have shown that rates of depression in teens who do not remember a time before the internet are skyrocketing. In addition, if we're reading the texts correctly, teens and tweens are maybe more anxious than ever. But studies like these are difficult, since the language teens use to describe their emotional states must be influenced by the language they use to publicly vie for attention, by that of their peers—and by that of anonymous trolls. In other words, as a parent of a ten-year-old told me, after reading through his kid's classmates' texts, "either they're all suicidal or none of them are."

If the hypothetical metaphor "the internet is a horror story" eventually beats out others ("the internet is water," "the internet is a building"), we would have another chicken and egg to ponder. Does the language we use to simplify complex concepts shape them, or is that language derived from the functions we most often see adjacent to those concepts? The internet, right now, is scary, and at the same time we might learn to swim through it, instead of drown.

To Be Fucked

If we have no gender, we have no women. Lately, we like the idea of obsession. Straight men are obsessed with sex, gay men are obsessed with form, women are obsessed with themselves, the internet is an obsessive habit. To catch a predator is to catch us all: we become what we least like about obsessives and narcissists when we spend "too much time on screens," although, like calling out a drunk for becoming "too honest," we can decide that this habit has made us our true selves.

I want life to keep going and refreshing and updating, and I want it to all stop and wait for me. When I got a phone with the internet, every single thing in my life changed. When I think about the internet (which is impossible), I feel similar to when I have a crush. I feel crushed. I feel like I have a crush on something, not someone, or maybe like I have an infatuation with everyone at once, but no one individually. I want to organize the people I know. I feel simultaneously like I miss every person I've met, and like I could go without seeing any of them again.

We don't want to feel like we've been advertised to and that it worked. So we say that we hardly think about it. We say that the internet and literature are separate, except that one can be found on the other. To ignore certain impulses that dictate our lives, and to write in earnest about living: Is this disingenuous? Is your relationship with the internet masochistic? Do you feel like it drains you of money, time, and dignity? Me too, and when I am trying to write, it taunts me, existing in the same space as the one in which I write, and choking my thoughts like a hangover. Maybe that's why it will be hard to write about how high it makes me feel when it does.

There have been some good examples of what I have such a hard time explaining, but I'm drawing a blank now, even though the internet is here and trying to help me. I'm thinking about Japanese coming-of-age movies, but from years ago, when the internet was a different place. Do you think that because I have no tattoos and have actually tried to delete contributions I have made to the internet that I do not understand the concept of permanence? Do teenagers scare you because they think of privacy in a different way?

The desire for success is intertwined with the desire to overcome, to establish, to become a fully formed person—in short, to come out. Will announcing a gender defeat you? Will you be burdened by your ordinariness? The desire for interaction becomes the desire to retreat. You need to be in a relationship to know your relationship status, which will deem you conservative, dependent. The desire for acceptance and love will be hard to separate from the desire for money, or, in its stead, online-notoriety. And this, too, has to be defined by a sexual preference. What do you like: to fuck, or be fucked?

The first thing you are taught when earning a teaching certificate is pedagogy. As a teacher, you must understand the teaching of teaching. How one imparts knowledge must be clear and challenging to a student. When learning about pedagogy you realize that you are being taught by teachers and their methods must be structured, but somehow they are not structured like the ones they are describing. The teachers tell you to teach in a student-centric environment, but you and your classmates have not been able to respond all hour.

In order to be recognized as an artist, one should make art, and this often involves attending an MFA program. In order to get into graduate school, though, one must prove he or she is an artist. It's like in the suburbs where you can't get a car if you don't have a job, and you can't get a job if you don't have a car. All anyone can focus on clearly is commercial success: Should you want it or reject it? Reject, obviously, if you have any integrity at all, but, professors tell you, you can have it if you'd like, and they know the people who can get it for you (they don't).

First, we discovered that women, all of them, felt underappreciated when given the tools to analyze their surroundings. Later, we learned that each woman has her own experience to recognize as devalued. Feminism, arguing for the understanding of every possible female trait and/or the proactive reconditioning of every young girl, rushes in and trips over itself, the fast-talking blowhard. The cultural reaction is to revert back to gender roles of another century, dreamily striding away from the debate arm in arm. The passive actors are not getting away with anything, though, and gender is less tangible than ever.

Describing a woman is impossible. I can say that a woman is different, but different from whom? I am not only speaking in a male voice, but in the voice of a male writer. The male writer is outspoken because he can be—his audience is listening, and in a male writer box, the echoes are even more meaningful than the cries. It is not anger he expresses, but sympathy for the female, the other. It is the future, he says, and we should not be afraid to look back.

In *What's Your Number*, a movie I've never seen, it looks like Anna Farris's character ends up dating only losers even though she's pretty and smart. The guy she needs is under her nose and he is criticizing her. She writes down the amount of men she has been with while sitting in a circle of other women and her number seems to be the only double-digit (nineteen). When everyone starts to read off their numbers, she tries to tear hers in half because she's so embarrassed.

On my way to a class I took on Czech literature at Charles University in Prague, I climbed a hidden staircase that led to a hallway full of empty cabinets squeezed abnormally close to one another. The classroom itself was an office filled with books about and by Kafka. There was a table only large enough for half the class to gather around, and the rest sat in chairs along the edges of the room, which was as hot and unventilated as the painter's "atelier" in *The Trial*. Our professor spoke about hierarchy when he saw us go for the table seats first.

I develop an accent through osmosis. Even when reading silently about a foreign country, one hears an accent. It is okay to say some words in the language from which they derive, but not others. An accent is much less committal than a dialect, but more offensive if used improperly. One cannot develop an accent abroad and later use it in their homeland for a longer period of time than the time spent abroad. One cannot use friends as an excuse but they can use parents as one. Often, people who have suffered severe trauma to the head or who have had a stroke develop an accent shades different from the one they grew up speaking. A new accent, the non-accent, is spreading: children who board in global village-like schools have a slow, careful tone and no recognizable origin other than tendencies towards certain words.

Czech natives, and Praggers especially, feel worldly because most of them have met so many tourists. They move to Prague because it is a big city. They are still intimidated by my Americanness, but I got the feeling that they knew they had a better sense of history. My country is young, and theirs has suffered more. "History repeats itself" is a warning for future generations, and it is one taken more seriously than religion. In Czech literature, each huge political movement was in reaction to the previous, seemingly more atrocious one. Which could do more damage: the aristocracy, or the proletariat? Which was more hateful: America, or Germany?

Czech writers love metaphors, and if what they believe is that people can only swing in one direction or another, hoping for a long break between reaching the hilts, the metronome in Letna Park (where Stalin's statue once stood) works perfectly as a metaphor for the whole city. In both directions there is cruel precariousness, but each extreme can be weighed out by its opposite. I learned that the statue of Stalin was blown up with dynamite and replaced by the red metronome, which illustrates not only the recursive nature of history, but the dependability of the passing of time. Czechs analyze each incredibly old artifact in their country in the same postmodern and cynical ways they do the new. They say the metronome is often broken. They also say that they considered replacing it with a statue of Michael Jackson.

First, I don't know how I can get so wet when I am this drunk (and I usually am). Second, I don't know why guys I sleep with tend to mention it. Possibly, they are frightened by it. I have even had complaints: "It makes for less friction," a guy once said. "There should be a perfect medium." This is something I didn't want to hear, but I asked him to continue. "A guy gets off on the fact that he is pleasing a woman, so he likes that he's getting her wet, but not necessarily the wetness itself." The wetness itself.

Both violence and the mundane are always coming up in Kafka's stories, repeatedly swallowing every other part of existence.

"This city makes me horny, and I hate it," said a fellow student who had cheated on his girlfriend with both a married woman and a Russian stripper. We were having beer and goulash alone together, but only because the rest of the group had left the restaurant to finish their final essays. I didn't know what to tell him because I knew that with this attitude, it was the beginning of the rest of his disappointments. Sex itself is almost recursive: a self-similar action that seems to transcend time and repercussions when it is happening, but only then. It is an act that creates a shared interest between people and a distinct self-image. Sometimes one does not want to see himself so clearly.

Teenagers are always a focal point in art and so we see recycled representations of adolescence, experimentation and failure in their freshest stages. Melancholy versus erratic behaviors, substance abuse versus fame obsession; all forms of angst are valid, and yet none are genuine or original. A fashion sphere informs each personality disorder, down to the language. As consumers we are in search of the most sincere of these faultily weighted emotions, because when we were teenagers, we felt like our childhoods were being taken away from us. The media had too much control over us, so we missed something, but we can find it in art.

A popular feminist troupe from the nineties gave a lecture about what every feminist lecture has been about since the nineties: The lack of female representation in the art world. They have had huge exhibitions in huge museums, and those exhibitions have criticized the very museums they were placed in. And the audience laughed at this fact, as if to say, "Those silly men, agreeing to put up your work. They have no idea." Attempting to create a movement that takes on inequality in the art world is farcical at this point, since the art world depends on the one percent. This new movement becomes part of the world, and it must, if it is successful, fall off the map and into history.

It is paradoxical to like the age you live in. Either you are told you are not seeing enough of the wrongs that are occurring, or you don't care. You must appreciate the past for its simplicity, and you must look forward to the future when equality happens.

"I tend to be attracted to large personalities," "I love gossip," "I'm bored," are supposed to mean you're a boring person, with nothing to offer the world. I am bored, though. My best friends are unbearable.

Narratives float towards the surface, using second or third person to tell a first person story, one about failure. Post a meme that points to the hypocrisy of everyone around you, and then post about the father of your child, about alcoholics in general, about how many places you've been today, how many games you've played, what achievements you've earned in this world, in a world that cares for you, you who are expected to care for so many who are careless.

The superhero is a popular metaphor for the outcast or minority, as is the diva. She is marked by her powers and she must stand alone, and therefore she is alone, and she must protect everyone else from their powerlessness. In the end, the more visceral, the more inexplicable, the more objectifying, the more passionately objectless something is, the more resonant.

The hero is worshipped, applauded, but also envied. Jealousy is the most poisonous emotion, and admiration is always laced with it. Wall Street is sacred territory to be protected, not a corrupt symbol of a system to be occupied. The terrorist and his minions—anyone who will listen to new doctrine, anyone who is ready for a change—creates a new effort towards chaotic violence. The garb of American train hoppers, a skinny brat crashing the climb of a big fish. We relate? We are not the libertines, nor the patriots. We are the critics. We grew up poor and hate the very poor; we want to be rich and hate the very rich.

Women sit in circles, we feel circular, we come around, we talk in circles, we don't get anywhere. A male orgasm and male genitalia: a line, a narrative. Female stuff: a circle? This line of thinking is getting me nowhere and I feel I need to start over.

I always liked Catwoman more than Wonder Woman, even if she is trouble, especially because she is trouble. Women are trouble, either because they have to be, or because they are. Batman sees something familiar in Catwoman. The difference between them is the difference between marginalized and not. Catwoman acts in a way that is more personal, intimate, and manipulative. This could never save the city. This could only save her.

Seven-Year Itch

Holly found out she probably had scabies before she could see or feel them. Giovanni told her she likely had them because he did, and because they'd slept in the same bed. He'd gotten them from sleeping in the same bed as Frank.

"We sometimes sleep next to each other," she said to the doctor. No, they didn't have sex, but they were close. "So, he got them from this guy, well, he slept in our friend Frank's bed, and Frank definitely has them, because he got them from his boyfriend, and his boyfriend's roommates all have scabies, and they keep passing it around. At least it's not bedbugs, though, right?"

"At least it's not bedbugs," repeated the doctor.

Until you've experienced an epidemic, it's hard to imagine how quickly and stubbornly things can spread. Maybe, for some people, it's hard not to imagine. Air is all around us, and so, if bugs too small to be seen are multiplying rapidly, they can be all around us, too. But it isn't like air, or water, or light, because invisible parasites are more difficult to close out or dry up or shut off and seal away.

Holly and Giovanni had been friends since she moved to New York for college. They'd met through other friends, uninterestingly. Coincidentally, Holly knew a few of the people Giovanni worked with, and Giovanni even knew a girl in Holly's Arabic Studies class. Coincidentally, Giovanni's grandparents had once lived in the small North Carolina town Holly for the most part grew up in.

Coincidentally, Holly had slept with one of Giovanni's friends, one he'd gone to RISD with. Giovanni had grown up in Connecticut. He'd known Frank since childhood. Coincidentally, Holly had slept with a guy that had been in Frank's band.

Scabies appear after about three weeks of contracting them. Well, the bugs are there the whole time, but the bumps pop up after two to six weeks. They are not bites, actually, but burrows. Scabies are caused by mites who live under the skin. Sometimes, you can see the patterns they make while crawling under there, dropping refuse. They tend to zigzag.

Giovanni was incorrectly diagnosed with dermatitis by his doctor, so he'd been treating his scabies with a thick cream called Triamcinolone for a few weeks. Giovanni was a tallish man with stretched dimensions: big hands, wide shoulders, long legs. He ran out of medication quickly. Again his doctor said it probably was because of the cold weather and the dishwashing job he kept that the tiny red spots appeared and reappeared around his wrists, his waist, and his ankles, and up the sides and the tops of his thighs.

He moisturized every day and applied the cream to the bumps, and then, when he went to sleep, usually next to Holly, he would take twenty milligrams called Hydroxyzine. The itching always got much worse at night, and so Marianne, his doctor, had prescribed this antihistamine that the information leaflet said was "used for the short-term treatment of nervousness and tension that may occur with certain mental/mood disorders (e.g., anxiety, dementia)."

Those ran out quickly, too, because Holly liked taking them. She would take only ten milligrams and sleep for ten or eleven hours, only dreaming of wonderful and realistic scenarios: her ex-boyfriend took her back and was interested in her research project for a computer science major; a friend she'd found attractive got in a fight with his beautiful girlfriend and whispered to Holly that he'd always liked her more; Giovanni took her sailing and every member of Holly's extended family was on a beach, waving as they departed.

Giovanni said he didn't have dreams like these, but that he could finally sleep without being literally woken up by itchiness. He'd tried putting cold wet towels on himself after showering, because the heat also caused more irritation, but he would always end up using the texture of the cloth to scratch harder, and sometimes the bumps would burst and bleed. They would seem much better every morning, and then worse than ever before, every night. He loved the Hydroxyzine, but it wasn't saving him. And Holly missed classes sometimes because she would sleep through her alarm's entire duration.

Heroin addicts sometimes see bugs crawling on their skin, and they complain to doctors in rehab facilities about it calmly and rationally. It is a phenomenon like any other related to drug addicts: their worlds are skewed from the chemical alterations in their brains, and so piecing things back together means shaking them clear. Like any puzzle—a jigsaw, a crossword, a Rubik's Cube, or a game of Solitaire—you sometimes have to take some pieces out to put the right ones in.

Junkies go to rehab to flush away drugs they've been so far diligent about keeping inside them. Sometimes you watch something happen so many times you just want it to keep happening, no matter what the results. The bugs and the night fevers and the shakes and the sweats seep out of the part that they've done—the thing they have pieced together and created—and yet, even if they've heard a million horror stories, the symptoms come as a surprise. It is surprising how inhibiting they are—more so, even, than that familiar, uncomplicated fiending.

Finally, both Holly and Giovanni convinced their doctors to prescribe them scabies medication: a thin cream called Acticin, which is applied to the entire body except for the head. Giovanni had had to point out to his doctor that the bumps were multiplying and showing up in the places scabies preferred: pulse points, armpits, behind the knees and in the webs between fingers and toes. They looked more and more scabies-like, too, now. The first batch varied in size and shape and depth. Now, each new one looked hard and perfectly domed, almost admirably so. Next to pimples and moles they were more uniform in color and size; they were so taut they were shiny, appearing in inconspicuous areas as if the bugs knew that they would persist if they could make themselves easier to hide.

Holly had had to tell her doctor at Campus Health that Giovanni's girlfriend, who lived in Boston, had complained of itching before she knew that Giovanni might have had anything, and that Frank, who lived in San Francisco, had spread it to several people. "Also, a girl I'm friends with in Los Angeles, who Frank doesn't know, told me she thinks she has it, and Giovanni slept with her a little while ago." The doctor asked again what Holly's relationship to Giovanni was.

Frank thought he was finally over his scabies about two months after he'd found the first bumps. He'd been incorrectly diagnosed at first, too. But he had a washer and dryer in his house, and he washed everything he owned, putting the stuff he couldn't easily wash in trash bags to suffocate the mites for seven days in a sunny area. He treated his skin and then re-treated at the end of the week. His boyfriend had done the same.

Two weeks later, symptoms were supposed to fade. Instead, they had intensified, and Frank went back to his doctor. She said it looked like he'd either caught scabies again or never fully exterminated his original swarm. Frank was not easily deflated. At least it wasn't bedbugs. He started the process again and finally broke up with his boyfriend. He washed his bedding every day this time, and treated his skin four times in one week. He never opened the trash bags and considered throwing them out. He bought all new underwear and socks and cleaned his fingernails and toenails every night. In all, he told Giovanni, it took about six months for the symptoms to completely clear from when they began.

Frank's love life was not as simple as he usually made it out to be, but then again, no one's was. It was easy to break up with that guy because it was easy to break up in San Francisco. It was easy to get dumped, too, if you had the right friends, who are waiting for your drunk rants about how he's gonna miss you more than you'll miss him. All the houses on Frank's street were tall and narrow and converted into duplexes and other things, with security doors in front of outdoor landings, or interior courtyards. Everyone could see Frank's ex-boyfriend crying sloppily in Frank's neighborhood that night, if they'd wanted to. But who would want to see that?

After work, Giovanni came home and found Holly studying. Their other roommates were out doing laundry because Holly had told them it would be a good idea but not totally necessary. She'd just washed the sheets and blankets. Scabies can only survive away from a host (human flesh) for a few days and they need prolonged contact to travel, and so you can only catch them, really, by sleeping in bed with someone. They are much easier to get rid of than bedbugs, which can lie dormant for up to two years.

Holly and Giovanni stayed in their underwear and stood near the heater in Holly's room. They applied the cream over themselves, poking between toes and scrubbing under fingernails, as recommended. It was hard to put it on the bottoms of their feet without getting dirt from the floor on their hands. They rubbed their hands like they were washing them, they massaged their own necks, and they inched the globs under their briefs and Holly's bra. They helped with one another's backs. Giovanni complained of a slight burning, but Holly felt nothing. She'd never suffered the itching, anyway, so it was hard to imagine the bugs under her skin being "paralyzed and killed" by the Acticin. They would shower when they woke up. They were supposed to keep the medicine on for eight to fourteen hours.

They got in her bed and continued the movie they'd started the night before, *Badlands*, in which Sissy Spacek plays a girl named Holly. It's funny how something like that can make the movies seem so much more personal. Holly watched as if she were watching a friend, proudly.

Afterwards, when Sissy Spacek would be brought up in a conversation, Holly would get the feeling you get when someone has brought up a person you know dearly. After meeting all the people she'd met in her entire life, it was hard to distinguish, sometimes, who she could make conversation about. Some people would make it easy: they would introduce you as their friend. Frank had introduced Holly as his friend to his boyfriend, and so she could talk about Frank as her friend, instead of a friend-of-a-friend (of Giovanni). And that girl Giovanni had slept with in LA. Holly knew that girl peripherally, and they'd had friends in common. They were friends online. When Giovanni and Holly went from San Francisco to LA in that rental car this last spring break, they'd gotten in touch, uninterestingly, and Holly introduced Giovanni to her at a party at which they all ended up. Now that she'd had a sexual connection to a person Holly had introduced her to, they were "friends." But everything is like that: not real until it is heard or seen. A box needed to be check-marked, even though, clearly, on a computer screen, all of those boxes have been filled or clicked or ticked, and Holly had over a thousand "friends."

She closed her eyes and inadvertently imagined the fast-motion crawling of the bugs under Giovanni's skin. Of course, this would be the most logically impossible time for her to get scabies from him. She would have already caught it by now, especially because when he slept, he'd itch the affected areas, then wrap his arms around her, placing his hands under her biceps. She imagined the mites and their larvae under his fingernails, crawling into her soft underarm flesh and around her nipples, which the leaflet said was a favorite area, too, but only on females. At least they didn't like vaginas. They did like penises, though, which Giovanni could attest to, and Frank could attest to fervently.

Giovanni was asleep about ten minutes into the movie. The poison on their skin should make sleeping this close to each other safer than ever before. But she'd never envisioned what was going on more vividly than now, after having read the information. "Can you sleep in your bed?" she whispered. He didn't move. She finally woke him from Hydroxizine-induced sleep with reluctant shoves, her hands covered in her own sheets, the ones she'd soon wrap herself with, anyway. "Can you sleep in your own bed?" she asked. "I feel gross."

"You are gross." It took an argument and some violent bed slapping and sheet pulling to get him out and into his own room. Holly imagined every part of the mattress he'd touched glowing with infection. It was an unhealthy scenario, their strange friendship based on wingman-ship, and she had known that for a while, but didn't think its ill fate could manifest into something so tangible.

Giovanni, once he'd gotten into his own bed, fell asleep and started to nightmare. He woke up sweating and called Kayla in Boston, who said she was too tired to talk. He fell asleep again and dreamt that the little hole on the top of a burrow on his wrist was big enough to see inside. It looked like the clear plastic on an Anatomical Man. Large tufts of hair grew behind his knees. He started to shave them off, and more clear plastic emerged, a window to oversized blood cells drifting along blue paths and soft pink tissue. It was beautiful, and Giovanni recognized this in the dream, while twisting with anxiety over his changing body.

He felt much better in the morning. Even if the itching persisted, and got much worse once he showered, rinsing away the Acticin, he couldn't help but feel he was starting anew. It would take a few weeks for the symptoms to disappear. What a funny thing to be worried about, anyway. This was the disease of crust punks and traveling street vendors—a gypsy rash. He walked into Holly's room, but she was already at school. She'd left the *Badlands* DVD menu playing on her TV, her laptop open, and her space heater on full blast. Instead of finding all the knobs and dials and buttons, he unplugged the whole power strip.

Giovanni interned at an art gallery. He noticed now if any of the patrons scratched. It was alarming how often people scratched themselves, or rubbed their shoulders, or adjusted their belts. The paintings on display were made up of silver pinpoints. Literally, someone had cut the heads off of millions or billions of pins. From far away, they looked like they were pulsating, like heat waves or computer screens on camera. Often art is described as reflecting the times. Are the times, thought Giovanni, indulgently, the plinth, or what adorns it? Perhaps every "time" is hedged in by its own reporting. Art reflected a tablet, and then papyrus, a newspaper, a carrier pigeon, and a flickering LED stock ticker. Maybe art never reflects, but projects the way people have to start thinking, because the news is just passing by so quickly, unquestioned, changing its very form before defining its own structure.

Like animals responding to climate changes, people faction off parts of their minds in order to streamline and condense, and so, there are squares on a screen called "pages" that we can "open" and "close." On the one hand, it's easier to draw a circle around everything one has and keep it in a tiny box, but on the other, it's now easier to see all the other possibilities. There are viruses and other messes that are more contagious than anything previously imagined. The presence of small dangers is so overwhelming, the dominant instinct is to diminish one's area and to constantly update it.

Holly, in class, wrote down lists. She listed items she needed to shop for, books she needed to read, chores she needed to do at home. What if she could just keep listing? She looked at the days of her iPhone calendar: She was going out with someone a friend was trying to set her up with on Friday. She was not nervous, just stressed. Would it be a waste of time? Could she make each day look full and promising by dividing the list up into the squares designated for days? Maybe she could have a folder for each day of the week, so she could separate the lists and assignments and phone numbers and medical emails, itineraries, museum schedules. Maybe she could make a folder for each guy she went out with. It was always nice to weigh their pros and cons, to see who had more in common with her, who seemed more like her father, more like her older sister's husband. No, not that, and not the other thing.

Dating apps probably were less creepy than they used to be. What was the difference between that and every other thing humans did to meet, anyway? If only every single aspect of life were like the tiny pills she took to sleep (which would run out soon, again). They were the tiniest pills she'd ever seen. She could put each partner, each goal, each lesson learned from a mistake into a pill and drop it into one of those plastic day-of-the-week containers or the glass-covered drawers of specimens in the science lab. It was obvious that Giovanni was a better friend than a lover, even if she had never been his lover. Still, guys get erections in their sleep all the time, so what did it mean that he'd never gotten one while lying next to her?

And what about all those girls he slept with, all over the country? He thought he could keep them happy by divvying up time and affection equally among them, filing them away and sending them neat postcards, in every city other than New York. But the one in Boston, Kayla, the only one he ever called his girlfriend, obviously had seniority. It didn't seem like a thing to be proud of, and yet it was, for Kayla. And yet, it wasn't all squared away like everyone thought it was. No. Because Kayla looked at Holly with menacing and exasperated eyes the last time she visited the city. Jealousy was the thing that would eat away at all the edges of everything, and make it all come ripping apart, surely. After class, Holly had a doctor's appointment. She had forgotten to put it in her calendar, though.

The average person with scabies actually only has about eleven mites in them. The term "scabies" refers to the affliction caused by the bugs, and not the bugs themselves. The bumps are where the females dig in to lay eggs, while the males roam on the surface, eating and mating. The itching is mostly caused by relatively massive amounts of fecal matter they leave behind. That's why it takes so long for the rash to go away, even after they are killed, and why it takes so long to start up, once they arrive.

The women Giovanni slept with regularly when he or they would visit were all always a phone call away, and his diffidence towards them almost guaranteed they would all answer him if he tried. He liked talking on the phone, about nothing, to these women, who either went to a state college or had to stay near an industry, like music. Frank, his best friend, was someone he called often, too, but they had never slept together. Holly was sexy in her own way, and sexier than a lot of these phone calls. Women always wanted to be told they were sexy, and he had never told Holly she was. Would she ever start asking him too, in the way that girls ask their girlfriends or gay friends?

It was for the best he had never slept with her, and they both knew it, because of their friendship, but also because he didn't shit where he ate, which meant he hardly fucked in New York. What a vast landscape of beautiful women gone to waste. But it was an unscathed landscape, and therefore all the more beautiful.

The process of networking here had already started, and he didn't want one type to merge with the other, because sex was messy, and he liked it messier than most, which was something he used to carry as a burden, opting, generously, for masturbation. But lately, more women preferred his type of sex, which had become a type, which he could easily search within porn sites. He wondered: What if Holly searched for another term? The possibility was simply too likely.

On his way home from the gallery, he knew what would make Holly laugh. He'd get *The Seven Year Itch* from the library. In the film, "the seven year itch" refers to the feeling Tom Ewell's character gets when Marilyn Monroe's character moves in downstairs. It's been seven years since he's slept with anyone other than his wife—the flat, hateful character hardly revealed on the screen. She isn't important.

Ewell finds the things Monroe says to be charming, even if they are dull and trashy. He fantasizes about their life together, listening to Rachmaninoff and having intellectual conversations, even though she doesn't know the difference between the penny novels he's paid to write and Dickens. Lust becomes his undoing and drives him hilariously insane. One can imagine him pulling out his hairs, one by one, trying to find the root of his misery. Why would life be made to scam him? Why would love have to end, and horrifically, with not a crash but a slow burn, interrupted by temptations of crisp, cool refreshment never to be experienced?

Giovanni walked through her door to find Holly with her face in her pillow. "Did Cynthia yell at you, too?" he asked, about their roommate.

"No, what?"

"Nothing. The rent. What's wrong?"

"Did you unplug my power strip?"

He looked at the wall socket, still empty, and at the strip, tangled in itself and in five or six chaotic wires. The plugs were in all states of disarray, some half-showing their metal nether-regions, pathetically reaching for quiet plastic slits.

Holly's voice didn't sound upset when she was upset. It sounded different than when she was not upset, though. "My fish," she said, still muffled by the pillow. She sat up and looked at him, wrinkles from the fabric on her cheeks. "You turned off their filter pump and they suffocated."

"I'll get you new ones," said Giovanni. He knew that Holly was likely a little relieved, that the fish were kind of a pain anyway, but

Holly said she didn't want to replace living creatures, that this was the wrong way of looking at things. "I'll get you something else then," he said, sitting on her bed. He plugged in the DVD player so he could insert *The Seven Year Itch*, but they hadn't finished watching *Badlands*. Holly's voiceover came on as the laptop started up again: "At this moment, I didn't feel shame or fear, but just this kind of blah, like when you're sitting there and all the water's run out of the bathtub."

Fashion

Bellwether Boots

At Balenciaga's Fall/Winter 2017 runway show in Paris, one model wore a loose, floral-patterned silk dress with unadorned red knee-high boots as richly saturated as the Soviet flag. It's a look that has become a signature for Vetements and Balenciaga designer Demna Gvasalia, who spent his childhood in the former Soviet Republic of Georgia. His then-close collaborator Lotta Volkova grew up in Novosibirsk, the third largest city in Russia. The two have made their influences well known—mainly, the contradictory styles that thrived in Eastern Europe after the fall of the Soviet Union. Theirs is a shared aesthetic that can be traced back to 1991, when items previously made scarce by the captive market, like American blue jeans, began flooding popular culture in eastern Europe. (The first big in-demand Vetements item was their reconstructed jeans—a collaboration with Levi's.)

The peculiar style of teenagers in the Eastern Bloc after the wall fell was a product of old world values accessorized with eighties Western sex appeal. Gvasalia has said that certain rose-printed plastic tablecloths in the Spring/Summer 2016 collection were an ode to his grandmother, and Balenciaga's Pre-Fall 2017 collection featured babushka-like bonnets. The Vetements trade-mark of an oversized, almost cheap-looking garment in traditionally feminine materials paired with something as emblematic of eighties Hollywood as red thigh-high boots explains it best: in nineties Russia, East met slightly dated West, creating a unique style all its own.

Gvasalia worked for Maison Margiela and Louis Vuitton before co-founding Vetements. The collective's first fashion show in Paris in 2014 was alarmingly influential; the tall, blank boots (an ode, in part to Martin Margiela's spandex stocking worn over pumps) soon flooded the feeds of fashion fans. Donatella Versace and Raf Simons at Dior tried styling seamless thigh-highs under drape-y dresses almost immediately—with caged metal-platformed stretch suede and Lucite-heeled patent leather, respectively.

But although the Versace and Dior versions were surprisingly similar in price, they didn't go quite as viral. Perhaps they didn't resonate as well as the high-low juxtaposition set up by Vetements (some of their styles have Bic lighters or road reflectors for heels); the slightly tacky sheen designed by houses at the top of the heap didn't quite cut through the luxurious feel of their surroundings the way the more ill-fitting underdogs did, looking like electric tape poking out from under the carpet—an exposed mask under layers of other stuff. In 2015, Gvasalia was named the new creative director of Balenciaga.

During the Fall/Winter 2017 month—meaning the official fashion weeks of New York, London, Milan, and Paris during February—the shapeless silhouette paired with extra-tall, relatively unadorned red boots was everywhere. 3.1 Philip Lim, A.P.C., Aalto, Adam Lippes, Aquilano.Rimoldi, Balenciaga, Emporio Armani, Erika Cavallini, Fendi, Francesco Scognamiglio, Giambattista Valli, Giorgio Armani, Isabel Marant, Joseph, Kenzo, Maryam Nassir Zadeh, Mulberry, Rebecca Taylor, Roksanda, Sharon Wauchob, Tomas Maier, Tory Burch, Valentino, and Zuhair Murad put tall, fitted red boots under billowing silk.

At Agnona, Calvin Klein, Céline, Christopher Kane, Ellery, Jil Sander, Jil Sander Navy, Krizia, Maison Margiela, Marni, Missoni, Miu Miu, Osman, Pascal Millet, Vanessa Bruno, Vanessa Seward, Victoria Beckham, Vionnet, Wanda Nylon, Y/Project, and each of Vivienne Westwood's labels, red boots were offered under boxy, eighties-like tailoring. Fenty x Puma and Yeezy paired them with tracksuits reminiscent of another Eastern European stereotype. One could have created a game of red boot bingo while scrolling through catwalk slideshows. Like clockwork, about halfway through each collection, there they'd be: fire-engine red streetwalkers peeking out from under a drab, almost comically conservative sheath.

"There is really nothing in the world that can be compared to red shoes," writes Hans Christian Andersen in his cautionary fairy tale, *The Red Shoes*. Here, a pair of cursed red shoes symbolize a poor girl's stubborn vanity. Eventually, she has to cut off her own feet to remove them. Kate Bush's "The Red Shoes" re-tells the story, making the pair—a gift from a fellow dancer—carry her to hell. The ruby slippers in *The Wizard of Oz* remind us that a heroine has "always had the power to go back to Kansas;" they remind us, too, of the jealousy and revenge waiting for all women: picture the Wicked Witch of the East's collapsed, curling feet that relocate those shoes to the wrong girl. In David Lynch's *Wild At Heart*, Lula is haunted by the idea that she would ever have to return to her broken home. All the same, when she is in danger, she clicks together her bright red kitten heels. As these characters try to go it on their own, they go too far. Maybe the most classic reading of the red shoe, then, is as symbolic of perilous independence.

In narratives, dangerous addictions to dancing and the too-high hopes of the displaced are metaphorically suggested with pumps and toe shoes made of satin. It's worth noting that a more recent influx of red shoes on the runway are made with less elegant materials that continue far past the ankle. They're not strappy or sparkly, but sturdy nylon and leather, kicking out from under drab khakis like secrets. In *Buffalo 66*, we see a nineties cult indie incarnation of iconic red shoes. Billy, too, has lost his footing in a blue-toned world of dirty snow and fluorescent lights, led astray before finding the love that was always within reach (with the girl he'd kidnapped). These shoes—an echo of ruby slippers, made in durable, seamless leather—are a more likely reference for the boots found on 2017 catwalks, which also appropriated plenty more from the nineties, an era obsessed with such contradictions as *jolie laide* (direct translation: "beautiful ugly"), heroin-chic, and sleeping with the (Cold War) enemy.

In the seventies, the Soviet Union saw reports describing smugglers being stabbed and robbed of black market jeans. The causes of this violence over so-called "Texan trousers" are disputable: American denim was very much in-demand, but it was also anti-Communist in that it symbolized Capitalism. In other words, if someone was jumped for their jeans, it could have either been a crime for fashion or a hate crime. Katherine Damm writes about the phenomenon in her essay "Soviet Denim Smuggling—The History of Jeans Behind the Iron Curtain."

"The simple fact that young people were so obsessed with any product contradicted Party ideology. Members of the older generation lamented the substitution of material goods for spiritual ones. Jeans culture was a type of philistinism, and slogans like 'prosperity without culture' and 'predatory consumerism' entered into anti-jeans rhetoric. Parents were chastised for indulging their children, and encouraged to talk to them about fashion in the context of their intellectual, moral, and social potential. Then, there was the nature of denim itself, known in East Germany as an 'embodiment of Anglo-Saxon cultural imperialism.' A 1979 *Guardian* article went as far as to say 'official Soviet doctrine has held that Western jeans, being figure-hugging, are a symbol of Western decadence, and thus to be avoided in the same way as pornography.'"

Those convictions didn't quite fall with the Iron Curtain, and the Russians who embraced Capitalist ideals in the nineties—if they could afford to—faced antagonistic audiences. New iterations of the specific style that emerged from this time period reference a disparity between ideal and real: Ideally, American styles were carefree, but in Russia, they were associated with pornography and prostitution. A tight, red, thigh-high stiletto boot worn under a one-size-fits-all dress easily captures this contradiction of American culture feeling dangerously ostentatious in the context of 1991 Russia. It is the marriage of a sexy red boot with a sack of a garment that propels the trend.

It's not quite as simple as dress-equals-Communism, boot-equals-Capitalism (the best fashion isn't that easy). Instead it works in the nineties' fascination with the ugly and the beautiful, or the Baba Yaga and the sexy spy Natasha. A sort of undercutting of frumpiness and androgynous Party dressing, this is a styling choice more than it is a direction for the clothing we later see in stores. (Styling, even more so than separates, conveys a collection's coherent message, if it has one.)

This use of the red boot, styled specifically to evoke tension, has the hand of Lotta Volkova all over it (besides Balenciaga and Vetements, she styled collections that showed iterations of the trend the same season: Mulberry, Emilio Pucci—where jersey sacks were worn with red heels and matching opaque stockings—and Kenzo), and so it's not a far leap to see the red of a communist flag against the gray scale of fatigues or the repurposed drapes of Cold War hit homes in these looks. The choice is especially provocative at a time when Russia was constantly on the front page of the *Post* and the *Times*.

This is fashion at its best, and its most frightening—a fashion that mines the past to predict the future. Before we heard conspiracy about the collusion of the White House with the Kremlin, we were—eerily—reminded of Russia's integration with globalized markets by way of retro looks. (American shoppers' interest in nineties Russia could be viewed as a red flag, so to speak.) Whereas hipsters in the Soviet Union, called "stilyagi," were criticized for wearing flashy American clothing that contradicted Communist ideals, our current interest in a post-Communist aesthetic is rebellious in a different way, layered as it is in nostalgia.

Which is why fashion lately is being pushed to self-consciously combat mass political ambivalence. There was likely never a fashion month so scolded for ignoring the political present than February 2017, the month that directly followed the inauguration of Donald Trump and preceded the UK's Brexit vote. Journalists called on fashion houses to use their platforms to raise awareness, or, in the cases of more youthful brands that typically work in themes of activism, to provide answers. Industry watchdogs weren't particularly hopeful. "New York Fashion Week: Vogue Runway's Editors React" asked, "How to begin a conversation about New York Fashion Week when the week itself seemed a bit of a nonstarter?"

Sally Singer explains, "I think I was not alone in hoping for style to have a more extraordinary response to the rather extraordinary times we now (sadly) live in. Buttons, slogans, and message tees are fine—they make pictures that are seen globally and register resistance—but they are not enough… One trend that I think will continue through Europe but I find peculiar in the extreme is the return of trouser suits that nod to Wall Street and 'mean business'... I couldn't help think how odd it is that that sort of tailoring would return just as the public's confidence in bankers and all implied associations has never been lower. Who is actually meant to wear all this suiting?"

One answer? The businesspeople who can afford luxury shopping—and who benefit from Trump's presidency. In fact, many shows seemed to quietly celebrate a political shift that favors industry over the causes that generally impinge on mass production, like environmentalism. In the same article, Maya Singer responds, "The semiotics of this trend worry me. Best-case scenario, designers are suggesting that we don the most useful disguise available, the better to infiltrate the power structure and enact subversions. But in a season where there was a lot of punting going on, I'm more inclined to believe this was an homage to the power structure itself."

Chioma Nnadi criticized Kanye West's collection for its Calabasas-centric "slogan tee for the 1 percent"—two months after West took a meeting with Trump. But reviews that followed sounded desperate for optimism, crediting certain collections with "irreverence" in the face of impending fascism, and making nods to "process" that apparently remind a consumer that "these things are *made*." Brands popped buttons in press notes, scrambling to align themselves with causes for social justice, while others, like Dolce & Gabbana (who often dress Melania Trump) celebrated an excessive style that once seemed tongue-in-cheek. Their runway show featured dozens of "influencers," mostly the children and wives of famous people. The clothing, as usual, looked like it belonged in the home of a Russian oligarch. *Vogue* editors called the show "inclusive" and "moving."

It's past the time we should admit that the fashion world can't solve political problems. As the designer for Prada and Miu Miu, Miuccia Prada—herself a former socialist activist in 1970s Italy—has said, "To be an opinionist as a rich fashion designer, I think is the worst possible thing to be."

This *is* fashion we're talking about. No matter how many American designers said, last year, that they would not dress Melania in protest of her husband's bigotry, many others announced that they would be delighted to see America's First Lady in their couture gowns. And no matter how many stores said they were pulling Ivanka Trump's China-made knockoffs from their racks (diplomatically citing "poor sales" and leaving the cause of sudden plummets for the shoppers to surmise), many others stated they would proudly continue to stock them. Either move, when put into words, is simply a PR one. While Ralph Lauren opted to vie for the most mentions via a credit for Melania's inauguration outfit, Marc Jacobs—not a likely choice for this type of event, anyway—used the very question of designing for the first family to publicly announce his rejection of possible affiliation. The timing, too, was political. Within days he showed his latest collection, influenced by hip-hop and titled, "Respect." (Surely he hoped we'd all forgotten the ire he provoked with a comment he made on social media last year defending his white models wearing dreadlocks by comparing them to black girls who straighten their hair.)

In fact, for Fall/Winter 2017, many designers commented on the state of things via branding, while others seemed to make statements about the absurdity of statement making, as fashion people. Instead of parading pleas for gender equality down the runway (as Maria Grazia Chiuri did in her first collection for Christian Dior by sprinkling t-shirts with phrases like "We Should

All Be Feminists" and "Dio(r)evolution" throughout a parade of tulle skirts), Prada fuzzed up the memories she likely had of her activist past, rendering it ridiculous by putting that style up for sale: Corduroy flares and knit bras were worn with crystal-embroidered mohair sweaters and jeweled satin heels. Famed seventies paperback illustrator Robert McGinnis collaborated on the collection by painting Bond girl-like babes on dresses and skirts. The message there was one about fashion and femininity: within both concepts, the past is in the past, and yet it haunts the future. How effective could those radical styles have been back then if we're where we are today? (About halfway through the show, a baggy silk dress was paired with knee-high red boots.)

But most fashion shows are a far cry from harnessing cynicism as adeptly. Some, like Versace, scrawled hopeful buzzwords on clothing ("Equality," "Loyalty," "Courage," "Love," "Power") alongside the brand's own blown up name, which could have rang inspirational in the context of Fashion Month but now reads simply as some throwback to Spice Girls-era pop.

Max Mara and Yeezy each cast Muslim model of the moment Halima Aden, a Somali refugee, and dressed her in a hijab for their shows. As *Vogue* noted, Aden's popularity was touching at a time when Trump made many Americans feel nervous about wearing religious garb. It should be noted, though, that the recent adoration from designers could be influenced, too, by the quickly growing percentage of Muslim shoppers in the widely suffering international luxury market. At the same time, Moschino tried to confront fashion's aversion to environmentalist efforts by creating trash-themed clothes—with no recycled materials. (And the ideas were blatantly derived from renegade up-cycler Margiela.) "Jeremy Scott for president!" wrote *Vogue*'s Nicole Phelps.

Calvin Klein and Vaquera made attempts at injecting one solid idea with another more culturally thematic one—each wrapped exactly one sagging American flag around a model—and in so doing, only directed attention to their own political impotence. Missoni included pink "pussy" hats in the final walk of its fashion show, and placed free samples on the seats of attendees. The move at least felt organic, since the hats are made in Missoni's signature zigzag knit. (Phelps: "feel-good moment of the week.") Still, those freebies are branded, high-end versions of homegrown beanies originally meant to inspire solidarity across cultural divides, like wealth disparity.

No one at *Vogue* seemed alarmed by Gucci's white-laced red combat boots that featured hammer-and-sickle insignias, the Cyrillic text in Heron Preston's (also hypocritically trash-themed) first collection, or the scissor-and-thread hammer-and-sickle on a new Stella Jean sweatshirt. Public School's red "Make America New York" baseball caps were baffling as items for sale: telling one apart from a "Make America Great Again" cap is impossible from a distance—and isn't it the point of those original caps to identify a Trump supporter from far range? The hats and the branded Balenciaga items in Bernie Sanders campaign font are all pastiche, part of a dressed-up scrapbook page of this era. They each take a theme seen in the streets and appropriate its design elements for another clientele altogether.

For Fall/Winter 2017, Gvasalia and Volkova let Balenciaga linger on the un-sexy Soviet in sexy shoes, but at Vetements, they'd moved on. Every look in the new collection was an unsubtle interpretation of an uncomfortable Eastern European archetype, modeled by people of all ages. Here was the commuting businessman, the struggling professor, the United Nations soldier, the policewoman, the rich old socialite, the black bouncer, the moped-riding university student, the midlife tourist, the sleazy broker, the homeless man, the pageant queen, the cowboy tycoon, the kinky secretary, the punk, the goth, the emo, the skinhead, the gabber, the club kid, the metalhead, the mail order bride, and even the Vetements fan. It was like the cheesy porno movie version of Russia—exactly the types of people we Westerners have been taught to think less of—on one of the hottest catwalks in the world.

The thigh-high red boots—still everywhere else—were gone. The one model in a floral print smock wore it over worn-out black booties and pants, under a hoodie cinched with a scarf. A mismatched track jacket was tied around her waist, as if part of a discreet getaway. Just behind her, a gray-haired woman was piled with synthetic skirts and overcoats, her purse strapped cross-body under the layers of cover-ups like she was afraid to lose it. There were no red flags here, only direct representations.

When the Vetements craze started a few years ago, the backlash was mostly incredulity—these were exactly the clothes of European migrants and mall-goers, said critics. Ever since, the designs seem to take a step closer to their references, not further away. While the red-shoed warning of dangerous independence was sounded everywhere else, the source of the trend said, "We're not in Oz anymore." Some have already clicked red heels and landed back in brutalist black-and-white, leaving the rest in a sea of colorful buttons, slogans, and pussy hats. This is no fairy tale, a parade of sad stereotypes and refugee costumes silently chanted. This is really happening.

Fashion Film

In 2016, yet another attempt at a funny, insightful film about the fashion world flopped. *Zoolander 2* was just a little too close to the real thing, perhaps. Not too real, really, but in bed with reality, featuring too many guest stars from the world it poked fun at. There was a miscalculation: no one ever wants the whole story spelled out.

Understanding *why* we desire—which, in a fashion context, can mean confronting the bleakly market-driven mechanisms by which trends are created—dissolves the longevity of want. Rather, the fashion world likes its films like it likes its own shows: an impenetrable arm's length away. We like our desires to be made complex by fashion, and vice versa. All the better if said desire is driven to desperation.

Does it come as any surprise that, time and again, creative directors list *Grey Gardens*, *Gummo*, or *Female Trouble* as having inspired their collections? Or that their top fashion icons are the female lead roles in *Basic Instinct*, *Taxi Driver*, and *Lolita*—which is to say serial killers, child prostitutes, and compromised girls? This is because discomfort, that tiny twist of perception that snags at one's moral compass, induces deep-seated desire. Women on the edge, in film and in fashion, stand in for impulsiveness, which is the goal of commerce. We want, and we display our wants, and we self-flagellate for wanting. Fashion is the portrayal of this cycle. We know that we're wrong to desire new clothes, but the desire persists. Eventually, the very same impulsive behavior that fashion inspires is its own icky inspiration.

That's where pseudo-celebrity and social media come in, vertebra to the ouroboros of consumerism. But fashion isn't history repeating itself. It is a study of history, and of identity as asserted through repetition. The most insecure of any art form, fashion takes into account every judgment being made and makes judgments of its own, recording the peaks and valleys of culture production. It is passive aggressive. Designers love to acknowledge their own disaffectedness, and at the same time, their self-imposed insulation from negative press. By design, fashion is elitist, and therefore will always necessarily be ugly and hypocritical. But this inability to resolve into some moral right or wrong is what makes it so irresistible.

The runway show is aggressively isolating. It has always been that way, and that was always part of the point. In the 1800s, a fashion "parade" was a presentation put on for the press and buyers: a sociological apparatus built around the promise of exclusivity. The shows were, in a sense, created as a presentation of hierarchy. Only the invited could see the clothing first, as it was being offered to them exclusively, in return for a better chance of placement both in the media and in stores.

The fashion show has drastically changed since its inception, and the validity of its original purpose has diminished. Among the more significant shifts is the invited audience. Those once solidly seated in the front row are assigned a place a few rows back, behind celebrities and influencers (once called bloggers).

In turn, the importance of attendance is increasingly being questioned. Brands are making their online projections instantly shop-able, slashing a traditional six-month wait time. So, what is being offered to physical show-goers that is not also offered to the millions of people who can watch the remediation of the show in real time? As Robert Altman's satirical look at the fashion world, *Ready to Wear*, noted in 1994 with its all-nude runway scene, we are there to see, up close, the emperor's new clothes. We are there to say that we were there. Although brilliant, this film flopped at the box office, too.

If attending a show were a statement of allegiance to a brand, why wouldn't every creative director then opt to make the show open to the public? Because large crowds don't gather for anything other than spectacle. So, if the fanfare is too difficult to achieve for a brand that is, instead of sensational, viable, why not do away with the show's seats altogether? Many brands are heading in that direction, slowly, by promoting real time looks at the collection before it even exits the backstage area, or staging a show for online viewers only by sending VR headsets for iPhones as invitations, etc. Runway shows have been live-streamed on and off since the nineties, but every season, some type of "innovation" is announced, wherein high fashion is purported to be even more within reach—a paradox: the promise of access to a world that is nothing if not elite.

When the fashion industry finally caught wind of social media, the response was mixed. Some fashion editors saw it as yet another front row to be seated behind. Others saw it as their chance to reclaim their courtside seats, and made sure their output was as close and as immediate as possible. Some brands scoffed at that strategy and instead refused to offer any type of social feed. Others started catering to a device-using audience by speckling collections with caption-like slogans.

Bloggers, trend forecasters, influencers, or whatever they will be called next have been partnering with high and low fashion brands for years, tossing back and forth the point of access for a shop-able look after researching optimal timing and placement. And as fashion viewers, we've been used to instant gratification for as long as street style photography has been as popular as runway reporting. When a straight-to-ecommerce option was finally consecrated as the future, it felt overdue. A scary sentiment in fashion.

No one in luxury seems excited about the quickly evolving process of promotion, embracing it like a phoney PR girl's air kisses. Immediate access rids fashion of some of its strange artificiality: each season, a team is tasked with recreating an imagined essence, another part of a brand's perfumed heritage. The runway show can be likened to the outrageous angel wings seen on those catalogue models lucky enough to be crowned Victoria's Secret Angels during the lingerie brand's own Christmastime catwalk show. The wings are never for sale. And in fact, much of a luxury brand's runway collections are not for sale, either. The moment a brand's real desire to be bought is exposed, the story unravels.

Just after the first "see now, buy now" shows premiered, the question on everyone's mind wasn't "How can I get those clothes?" but, "How well did the plan work?" As the sales statistics were brought into focus, the strategy was clearly one that, on the self image smoke-and-mirrors front, wasn't particularly concerned by the threat of failure: were there to be no scandal in the numbers, no one would care.

The shop-the-runway model promises exclusiveness, justifying this verbiage by giving customers a limited time to buy, before everyone else has in-store access. But a privileged or advanced shopping time slot is generally not how fashion defines "exclusive." Luxury is still only as luxurious as it is unreachable, by way of cost, self-selected offer, and brand status. And that status, as decided by the rest of the world, hinges on a ratio of confidence to solvency—in other words, a level of risk multiplied by real desperation. Even if the fashion world is headed in the direction, shop-able runways are still case studies. They could actually fail by giving VIP access to everyone—rendering no one very important at all.

But at the core of big brands' plans for infiltrating online shopping, a self-aware human center can be detected. Branding (including anti-branding branding) is essential to online shoppers, because it is difficult to find value in an image of a product on a screen unless it very clearly speaks of its luxury provenance.

If what's trending now is at once a reprise of late nineties logomania, like Louis Vuitton and Gucci symbols, and a continuation of the anti-capitalist reaction to it, like chalky, drawn-on Chanel logos and Adbusters-ish faked brand-alliances, like Hood By Air's Paramount Pictures mock-up and Vetements's Champion sweatshirts, then Maison Martin Margiela, the house founded in 1988 that, by attaching a plain white tag inside garments with four thick white stitches (easily seen on the outside), basically invented anti-brand branding, is the biggest influence on today's runway scene. Martin Margiela, throughout his career, remained hidden, un-interviewed, and un-photographed. His strict anonymity came to represent a mythological human spirit behind luxury consumerism, the antithesis of influencer marketing and empty hype. Still, only the trademarks of his brand (the tag stitches, the Tabi shoes) remain bestsellers.

Fashion that transports a consumer eager for innovation must place that uncomfortably desperate feeling, a waggling tongue, into its cheek. It must reflect the unease of society, as did the small town metal fans in *Gummo*, the upper-crust outcasts in *Grey Gardens*, or the fame hungry high school dropouts in *Female Trouble*. And as Margiela did, by constructing garments from everyday objects, or as Jean-Paul Gaultier did, by placing the inside materials on something's outside, it must see the way things are.

And what defines our time, generally? We are celebrity-obsessed and all celebrity candidates; we are being surveyed and surveilled, our opinions exploited via our own narcissistic tendencies; we are afraid of attacks and paranoid about the ways these attacks are being explained to us; and we are, as always, hoping to appear sexier than we feel.

Dysmorphia is inevitable in self-imaging, and the runways compound it. Here are stories of reshaping a self: the fetish costume, the office uniform, glamorized sportswear. These tropes invoke intimidating standards, dreams of a status painfully out of reach. What they create is not activewear made for gym use, but sports-influenced eveningwear, with nods to the uniforms of professional teams and corporations. It's up to us to imagine what game is being played.

Many a fashion writer has linked the rise in wearable tech to the rise of the surveillance state, runways providing the masses with armor to protect their selves from a pervasive government eye. But high fashion has never truly been where a practical item is unveiled. More than anything, runways reflect a metaphorical us, just as we are.

Tech, athleticism, and exhibitionism as themes in fashion reflect the rising popularity of gym enthusiasts at the same time as social media has made the act of working out a much more familiar enterprise. Workouts are sexy because they affect vulnerability, they tell a classic story of struggle, and they involve tight clothing. People "like" gym selfies. The equipment seen in them isn't new, but the access they represent is. Sexy, non-sweaty workout photos are surreal: everyone's makeup is pristine and exercise looks easy (defeating the purpose of exercise, we can assume).

I asked my Facebook friends which garment they most often see on Instagram that they never see in person, and the overwhelming response was "waist trainers." So when, at a DKNY runway show, I noticed that the collection looked sporty, yet cinched, I thought of social media celebrities selling ineffective athletic accessories, even if the reviews used words like "utilitarian" and "New York nineties street style." Off the runway, in the real world, a silk dress with thick laces looks far more couture than varsity. If done right, it is an inside joke about the way sports and uniforms—symbolic stand-ins of an absence of individuality—make us, the fashion victims, feel. Memories of trying to fit in perhaps, as someone more interested in art than in competitive sports, comingle with the classic reactions to a soft silhouette.

Fashion, unlike painting or sculpture, can't stray too far from the body if it wants to make an impact in its designated venue (the stores). A designer cannot completely forego evoking feelings of sexual desire if their aim is marketability.

"The greatest intensity of sensual passion," Freud said, "will bring with it the highest valuation of the object." Our sexual desires, intensified by our insecurities, are easily conflated with shopping urges. The mind steps from loss to want, from depression to unrequited love. Sex is fetishistic. Sexiness is competitive. When clothing is sexy, it straddles the line between desperate and desirable, each direction causing a type of frenzy.

Later in 2016, another fashion film, *The Neon Demon*, flopped. The horror movie stages fashion photo shoots that are hard to differentiate from other scenes and casts mostly real models as models. Admittedly, it is as campy as any fashion favorite, its very theme being desperation, but perhaps like *Zoolander 2* and *Ready to Wear*, its substance is too close to its own target—a dangerous place to be because in the fashion world, where the line between fabulous and tragic is as fine as the thread in an emperor's robes.

Good-looking People

My introduction to Abercrombie & Fitch was also my introduction to an all-white high school, Calvinism, and the Dutch Christian Reformed Church. At fourteen, my family moved to a Midwestern city full of winter sports and summer lake houses. Even the punks were religious. Here, I was confronted with a style that so far did not exist in my childhood but was a determinant throughout the childhoods of my new peers.

My new ninth grade class wore their Abercrombie with chunky brown low-top Doc Martens, hooves on horse-like creatures. Everyone was blonde, athletic, and impeccably groomed. In my mostly Mexican middle school, girls wore name brand clothes, too, but from sneaker stores, skate shops, or Playboy. There, pants were wide-leg or sewn up to be skinny, never boot cut. I had imagined what teens in the Midwest dressed like and was way off. I was fascinated by the ugliness of Abercrombie. It was clearly a cult, and I had an uncompromised outsider perspective on it.

In 2006, then-CEO of Abercrombie & Fitch, Mike Jeffries, said that sex appeal is "almost everything." He went on to say, "That's why we hire good-looking people in our stores. Because good-looking people attract other good-looking people, and we want to market to cool, good-looking people. We don't market to anyone other than that. In every school there are the cool and popular kids, and then there are the not-so-cool kids. Candidly, we go after the cool kids.

We go after the attractive all-American kid with a great attitude and a lot of friends. A lot of people don't belong, and they can't belong. Are we exclusionary? Absolutely. Those companies that are in trouble are trying to target everybody: young, old, fat, skinny. But then you become totally vanilla. You don't alienate anybody, but you don't excite anybody, either."

Although it wasn't smart of him to say this, he was right. Even the brands that don't strive for mainstream cultural capital face the problem of losing sight of their target audience once they lose control of advertising strategies. The goal for a fashion label is to make a brand iconic, and to sell the iconic feeling to a person who can afford to pay too much for it.

Since its start, Abercrombie was never classified as a luxury brand, and it wasn't even very expensive, just slightly more expensive than similar mall stores. In its late-nineties heyday, it was the brand that made sexy versions of the clothes kids already wore to school: T-shirts and jeans, stuff you could toss a football in or throw on the grass if everyone decided to go skinny-dipping. It was better than the cheaper versions of this because it advertised a name that said fitness, youth, and casual sex. A&F was not snobby country club attire or logo-less workwear, it was somewhere in between. More importantly, it was for those who were casually peaking in high school.

Every kid in my new school had a Starbucks Frappuccino in their cup holder. Imitations were statements, too: Redbull's sleek can was coveted unless you were part of the alternative Monster crowd. Whereas caffeinated drinks signified coping mechanisms to get through the torturous day before one's better things to do, clothing had to appear to prop one up with affectless comfort. Trying too hard was punishable by ostracism. A&F had the brilliant plan to become a top-tier lifestyle brand situated in the empty space just above thrift store grunge, which had lost some relevance once it was co-opted by high fashion.

When *A&F Quarterly* was born, it was packaged like porn, in brown paper, and shipped to tweens and teenagers nation-wide. Sex scenes photographed by the infamously erotic Bruce Weber influenced the first feelings of arousal in many a Midwestern pre-teen, gay and straight. Perhaps, they thought, blissful, perfect sex was available at camp, or in back yards. *A&F Quarterly* was made up of athletic bodies unlike the heroin chic models walking runways. They smiled, laughed, and posed in goofy scenarios, possibly the result of alcohol or a dare. Men pinned down other shirtless men, clothes got pulled beyond repair, and everyone got pushed into the pool.

Parents were upset about their kids seeing softcore porn, and as a result begging to buy the clothes associated with it at the mall from a nightclub-like store, bumping bass-heavy music and guarded by hard-bodied greeters. This was before the internet was accessible enough for us to search hardcore porn, or fast enough to get a full experience with it. A&F became something parents warned their kids against, making it even more desirable. Thus, the lifestyle brand—complete with fragrance and friendship bracelets—was, at its height, as popular as it ever wanted to be, only worn by the cool kids. Theft was no big deal: the sales made up for that, seeing as A&F merchandise was priced higher than the company's cheaper, almost identical lines.

Kids in my high school wore shirts that read, "Wok-n-Bowl" and "Wong Brothers Laundry Service: Two Wongs Can Make it White," accompanied by cross-eyed propaganda-style cartoons. If you weren't part of the in-crowd (and white), A&F was oppressive. Non-jocks made their own anti-A&F T-shirts, using the brand as a catchall for exclusionary, competitive behavior and old-fashioned bullying. Now, ironically, knockoff A&F is a popular Chinatown look. Reclamation of the brand may be calculated, but often this exact trajectory is unplanned. The controversy caused by sexism, racism, and elitism gives a brand enough mileage to perform its next stage, in novel contexts.

Similarly, golf and polo outfitters Tommy Hilfiger and Ralph Lauren became so knocked-off and collected by a more urban crowd that new versions of the brands were launched specifically for the plagiarists. These strategy adjustments came with growing pains. There was that rumor that Tommy Hilfiger himself said he hated black people wearing his clothes, and there were the Lo Lifes—a subculture made up of people who exclusively wore Polo and reportedly never purchased it. There was also that quote from a spokesperson for Cristal champagne in the *Economist* about rappers promoting it as part of a "bling lifestyle"—"What can we do? We can't forbid people from buying it"—and Burberry's alleged annoyance with the middle class adopting its plaid signature. The strategy of exclusion isn't itself necessarily racist, but designers and CEOs themselves usually come off as racist, probably because they are.

In my white high school, like so many scenes from eighties-onward movies suggest, there was a class system. Cafeteria tables were designated into small groups, and the most popular of these played sports, but liked beer. They were motivated enough to board a pontoon boat at dawn in the summer, but relaxed enough to enjoy the next several hours floating on it. These were the Abercrombie kids: snowboarders, date rapists, and class clowns, slightly less passive than the stoned skaters.

They needed specified branding, and A&F's was so on-point, it's mentioned repeatedly in the 1999 hit by boy band LFO (Lyte Funky Ones). "Summer Girls" was a checkpoint for a generation, made up of pop-culture references. To everyone who hated A&F, the brand represented the staggered systems of upward mobility and whitewashing. Abercrombie wearers were a group who ridiculed gays (despite the catalogue's sensual poses), minorities, the overweight, the pale, and even the super thin. The brand was, like the boy bands and girl groups of the time, an all play and no work clique, sexy and blissfully stupid.

Popular movies of that time were teaching kids to be wary of grownups. *Teaching Mrs. Tingle, Disturbing Behavior,* and *The Faculty* depicted evil adults, perhaps making us more fearful of aging than the preceding generations. The most rebellious former hippies all seemed to end up working for the Man, fearful of the free expression of rap music. The grownups, only around to break up the fun, were shown in movies as lurking in the shadows. Yes, it was only the dumbest of teens that couldn't see that the industry apparently protecting them from the evil adults were adults themselves—and the most evil out of everyone, owning sweatshops and committing fraud. But the dumbest teens also turned out to be the hottest.

In 2006, it was discovered that Lou Pearlman—manager of the Backstreet Boys, NSYNC and LFO—was running one of the country's biggest Ponzi schemes on record. And by 2006, Mike Jeffries' most controversial public statement on sex appeal was really just saying what we were all thinking: "Are we exclusionary? Absolutely." Those remarks were followed by lawsuit after lawsuit, mostly involving staffing discrimination. An announcement about the store refusing to carry anything over a size ten reportedly marked a noticeable decrease in sales.

A&F couldn't stay popular forever. In 2011, wearing A&F became an ironic statement for artists. Tumblrs, DIY photo shoots, and performance art projects were devoted to defaming the brand by having an "outsider" wear the clothes. The brand stole its name and rustic identity from a bankrupt fishing and sporting goods company founded in 1892, but A&F as we know it started in 1988. It was almost immediately copied by other mall stores like American Eagle and Aéropostale. And then came the A&F knockoffs—a fate the casual luxury brand once assumed they could avoid.

Eventually, A&F stopped being trendy, as trendy brands do. Its fall from grace was a signal to those it had deemed unpopular to adopt it. In other words, the people A&F had once intentionally excluded became the only ones interested in it. Small news items suggested that people were still outraged by every little thing A&F did, which likely confused the company into thinking that they still had sway. In 2013, some Taylor Swift fans reacted to a shirt that read "#more boyfriends than t.s." A&F pulled it from their stores. Never mind that the shirt's message, in trying to be relevant, missed the mark by making up a hashtag with spaces and punctuation (every Swiftee-age internet user knows that a hashtag broken up is a hashtag broken).

But despite its rumored collapse, A&F persists, the same way American Apparel, after all that talk of bankruptcy and sexual misconduct, somehow stayed open for years, and then reopened with a new name. AA's clothes were similarly innocuous and well-branded. Both brands cornered a customer uninterested in fashion but intent on looking good.

Although A&F the company had an idea of who they wanted as customers, their fantasy world became too enticing. The idea was to limit wearers to the privileged middle class youth by capping the sizes offered, blatantly appearing racist, and loudly proclaiming their target. But A&F *the image* presented many outside of that target with a sexual awakening. Instead of creating a style that was at once reachable, desirable, and elitist, A&F inspired horny teenagers to co-opt it. Two decades later, wearing the "All-American" made-in-China brand, for all its failings and truly American flaws, somehow looks subversive.

The Micro-trend

A micro-trend, as I understand it, doesn't last the time it generally takes to be recognized as a proper trend. It burns out because it flares too brightly, too quickly. But micro-trends are often what later inspire larger trends. Something that was too blatant or obvious to become fashionable at its inception can later be re-contextualized as a relic and ultimately become a signifier of its era. And this has always been the case. Almost without fail, the least chic trends of a decade are revived twenty years later.

Lately, contemporary reportage has micro-tized many trends with proper potential. In other words, dynamiting infant trends microtizes them. This process is now easier than ever.

Being short-lived is not the only factor that makes a trend micro. The trend may be followed too wholeheartedly by one age group, for example. It could be a cheap accessory that started too low on the supply chain to trickle back up to high fashion its first time around. A phenomenon could be bubbling underneath a broader fashion narrative for some time before it is discovered as something even slightly tangible. Take a *T* magazine article from July 2015 about dyeing armpit hair. The story goes: Manic Panic colors are in style for armpit hair this summer. Actually, as anyone knows, this is an uncommon practice with obvious setbacks, and one that can really only be sustained as something—quite literally—cool, in images.

"The internet, it turns out, is up to its armpits with women who dye theirs," the article insists. "Miley Cyrus displayed her newly pink underarms in a photo she posted to Instagram, drawing more than 396,000 likes and more than 30,000 comments. On Instagram, more than 700 photos of women (and a handful of men) have been posted with the hashtag dyedpits. And a blog post by Roxie Hunt, a Seattle hairstylist, 'How to Dye Your Armpit Hair' has been shared more than 37,000 times since it was published in October."

Trusting these numbers when it comes to fads blatantly ignores the information that journalists tend to keep in mind when it comes to anything else. Another article claims that keeping track of emerging hashtags is important because "#normcore was the most Googled trend of 2014," insinuating that because something is Googled a lot, it makes a big impact on the economy and fashion. When a pop star's post gets a lot of attention, the content of the post is still not necessarily a trend. And that something as unusual as a woman putting semi-permanent color on a body part notorious for sweatiness is a topic shared by many, that does not necessarily equate to a group of people following these instructions. It simply makes the topic a trending one.

The first sign that people don't really understand how these things work is that they treat the internet as if it were a place. Take the meme heelconcept (to be differentiated from a micro-trend by its very deliberate countercultural intention). Rolling its eyes at prevalent phenomena ranging from photographing high heels to the emergent obsession with bedroom life on social media and a forced aesthetic connection to feminism, the heelconcept bluntly negates the frenzied discussion of fashion trends. Examples of the meme place a foot in a still life that loosely represents the shape of a high heel that could never become an actual high heel. No strap holds the structure to the foot, or the heel is made of liquid, or the shoe is rooted to the ground. No designer could steal these concepts without bastardizing what made them so evocative—that they are part of the outside world, staged on taupe wall-to-wall carpet, using drugstore products, and are impossible to place on a walking model. They are not a part of the insular fashion world, nor do they want to be. They are untrendable fashion.

If a trend can come and go before a magazine has time to print it, perhaps it was really an event. Since social media started, runway shows that are put on a whole season ahead of time sometimes end up accidentally dictating the current season. That's because the world can see everything in fashion as it is happening, not months after, in the ads. Of course, it's all one and the same. A micro-trend—like dyed armpit hair—is still part of the fashion cycle, and always has been. The styles seen on runways borrow from concepts found in micro-trends or untrendable fashion, which come from Instagram, and before Instagram from clubs, raves, protests, secret societies, the suburbs, etc.

The runway has always been late in this way—and magazines even later—although both are often sourced as a trend's earliest sighting. That's fashion's job: answering to, solidifying, or codifying something that's already in the air. That thing is then translated into clothing, or it's co-opted by a pop star, a store display, a *T* article. The message—now formed by a group of contributors over time—has made its way to more than just the ether. In its nuanced anarchism, the heelconcept, for example, is woven into the fabric of a larger trend; it assumes a mood that is a reaction to—not an iteration of—so-called street style.

Another article I skimmed listed a few "Instagram stars" who have worn bonnets in selfies. "Is #bonnetcore the Next Big Street

Style Accessory Trend?" it asks. Most of the images in the slideshow are taken from Instagram, and they show sarcastically pouting people—like actor/artists Jake Levy, Lauren Avery, and Lily Rose Depp—in staged pastel portraits, not caught on the street outside a fashion show.

Another article I half-read the other day mentioned that babies might be trending, because they were showing up a lot on runways. Another one, "Mourncore: Hot New Trend or Something We Invented on a Summer Friday?" And "Individuality is Trending." A response piece to bonnetcore called out those reporting on and tagging "trendlets" (including plastic bag onesies and heart-shaped hair selfies), saying that because of the way they're blasted out, they're always exhausting, and that naming them a trend immediately kills them. Strangely, this article made sure to point out that normcore, in contrast, is "very real."

A prevalent trend I've noticed in fashion lately is that journalistic integrity is something now deemed outmoded by brands and corporate-run magazines, and that the readers are pissed off. Trending now is outrage at trend forecasting. Backlash is never far from any trending topic, although this particular type of backlash, or meta-trend, is fraught with self-loathing. Those who point out that new ways of reporting are too intertwined with attention seeking to be trustworthy are invariably seeking attention themselves. One upset op-ed demonizes the rest, and it all starts because someone at an aggregation site had to post a certain number of articles per day and gain a certain amount of traction over time. No wonder the natural impulse for writers forced to create content every few minutes is to focus on something as serene and simple as bonnets and babies.

It's not that fashion has actually become faster. "Fast fashion" is certainly a problem: it puts a greater stress on the system of irresponsible labor practices and depleting natural resources in the fashion industry. It might seem logical to blame this on the internet's quick proliferation of fashion trends. But trendiness has not become a bigger priority over the past few years. The idea that people (meaning a relatively large percentage of the population) go wild over some newly announced street style phenomenon is inaccurately reported. Over the past decade, the only difference that the internet has made in terms of how we view fashion trends is to illustrate the industry's ill-intentions. The internet has helped reporting (of anything) become easier to monetize, and so sensationalist journalism has become accepted.

This is due to a shift in the way we view our media. We filter it through our friends. If our friends can get us to look at something easily, advertisers want to make sure our friends are sharing their stories, whether via a site with which the advertisers are affiliated or through a direct link to a product. Trends, just like all trending items on our feeds, must somehow seem to be at a critical mass to become newsy enough to be shared. Bonnets are not trending, but still lifes are, because Instagram is. But it won't be forever. That space, too, is a meta-trend (a mega-meta-trend). It's something that overwhelms the industry of trend forecasting, fashion, and art and yet is a trend itself. Trends are trending. Isn't it boring?

Another article I read awhile ago purported to be an essay about shifts in personal style. It argued, I think, that because it is easier to acquire clothing almost immediately after discovering it, and because clothing production now allows for a wider array of specific trends made for mass consumption at low costs, personal style is becoming more personal. This view seems narrow, seeing as it relies almost completely on cheap labor. Personal style can never, in fact, become more personal. It can only become more widely known as one's own.

When it comes to assessing fashion before and after the advent of the internet, it's the coverage that's changed the most. Fashion coverage has a different texture than the once-a-month trend forecasting from the heyday of print magazines. Personal style platforms have become more financially successful than most magazine websites. Compared to the web component of an existing print magazine, personal brands have small overhead and are so far viewed as more trustworthy in terms of styling and advice—meaning that readers have become wise to magazines' relationships with advertisers, while an influencer's product placement negotiations are harder to spot.

Traditional brands notice personal brands and their influence; they notice the importance of street style and social media, and they pay attention to e-commerce source links. Magazines, with their meetings and mastheads, are decreasingly a part of the fashion trend equation.

As a periodical, a magazine becomes a capsule of the cultural climate. Some magazines, having always known this, become the best stethoscopes for fad pulse-points and, later, the best references of a time period. They will attempt to recognize a micro-tend before reporting on it, and jump to no conclusions. Some trends are best left ignored until they are blazing in full glory. The rest, even those with decades of cultural relevance, cave to the contemporary pressures of guaranteeing their advertisers a flash flood of views. These, like so much media, will not burn out so much as fade away.

The Scammer

Scambaiting is a term used to describe the action of scamming a scammer, in particular a 419 scam perpetrator. The 419 scam, also known as the Nigerian Prince scam, refers to Nigeria's fraud criminal code. Even though the percentage of advance-fee scams coming from the country of Nigeria is relatively low (the United States is the biggest perpetrator, says Wikipedia), this particular type of fraud has become synonymous with Nigeria in popular culture, and scambaiting forums primarily ensnare Nigerians. Websites like Scamtacular and 419 Eater provide open boards for scambaiters to discuss and post evidence of the humiliation inflicted on African men in small towns. It's difficult to parse out who is being victimized in these scenarios. The rhetoric used on scam websites' mission statements gets conflated, and a reader is left questioning everyone's motives.

419 Eater says, "You enter into a dialogue with scammers, simply to waste their time and resources. Whilst you are doing this, you will be helping to keep the scammers away from real potential victims and screwing around with the minds of deserving thieves." Wikipedia says, "It is, in essence, a form of social engineering that may have an altruistic motive or may be motivated by malice. It is primarily used to thwart the Advance-fee fraud scam and can be done out of a sense of civic duty, as a form of amusement, or both."

Like with Anonymous, Wikileaks, and other vigilante groups who use internet back alleys to distract or jeopardize the actions of other groups, so-called anonymity can lead to witch hunts. And as we've all learned, most people's manners go out the window when shrouded by social media's diaphanous cloak. From the first sputters of cybering, chatroom dialogue, and dirty chain emails, we found out that talking to strangers via web brings out a side of us over which we have less control than is comfortable. And as we climb the steps of new modes and routes of communication, we see the fascinating side effects—mainly, abuse.

Scambaiting is unethical because it is exploitative. Then again, it Robin Hoods its victims, evidently all scammers. It is illegal in most public places to beg for money, but not to give, even though handouts end up being the necessary fuel for much crime. The roles of hero and villain, here, are skewed from the get-go: The photographic evidence of the scambaiters' projects largely targets Nigeria, a country the mainstream media has disproportionately associated with hustling. Via email, dating apps, and physical letters, Nigerian Prince scams (and many other types of scams) have robbed the trusting and the elderly. The conversation is further complicated by guilt. While reading emails from "large estates" asking for our cooperation in transferring funds internationally, one can imagine the emailer's desperation, even if one is not tricked by the story being told.

Just as often as an email scammer is someone with a foreign-sounding pseudonym living in a distant country, one is a Craigslist potential roommate, or a phoney relative with a fatal disease. And no one is immune to every scam. None of us want to find ourselves questioning a scam on a day when we don't feel quite like ourselves. Anyone can become what we hate or desire or fear in commentary and retaliation. And unless we are being scammed or traced, no real damage is done to our own egos when we feel that all we have put out is feedback.

So, what if we put out more than feedback, something contro-versial, of our own? A letter to the editor, a video response, a viral campaign? If a feedback loop forms, we can predict rapid escalation from negativity to bigotry. The internet is vast, and only the waves with the highest peaks are noticed. The immediacy with which the most intolerable testimonies are answered gives rise to new forums for the purpose of unsolicited discussion, which makes more room for argument and verbal abuse. Once the blasé and the neutral are whittled away from the sphere of commentary, we're left with a net-work of primal pissing contests. The attention paid to the extremes feeds the extremists' need to constantly and consistently self-publish.

Apparently, the advance-fee scam (in which a letter from a stranger asks for an advance or bank account information in order to free up a large sum of money, a percentage of which the letter recipient is promised, in exchange for participation) dates back to the late eighteenth century, and likely originates in Europe. Popular versions of the scam came from Spain and Germany, targeting widows of war and lower class citizens to whom a relationship to the aristocracy could be suggested, among others. The racializing of the scam is typical to American culture: white people here tend to wildly inflate the crime rates of people of color. For example, the term terrorism is associated with Middle Easterners, when more crime sprees in this country are caused by men of European descent, by a large margin.

Online and otherwise, we dress in drag. We hide our sinister emotions and biased conclusions. We wear representation of our real selves, perhaps especially in internet-only communication. Exploitation of this instinct is tricky. Scambaiters snare their scam-mers and ask them to pose in traditional drag, holding signs that insinuate that the scammers are being forced into homosexual encounters. The scammers are performing for the audience of scam-baiters, supposedly letting their greed annihilate their dignity. But the scambaiters are performing, too, for the audience of the scam-baiting forum and for the scammers they have targeted for humiliation. Scambaiting involves as much trickery as the original scam it foils. The performers are now involved in a dance of lying, persuasion, and goading. The photos on 419 Eater show a strange comfort in the performance. The scammers must know English if they are communicating with English speakers (the official language of Nigeria is English), and they must see the disconnect between money laundering and homoerotic voyeurism. Are the photos fake? What would a faked photo shoot of a Nigerian scammer entail?

Thus goes our online-only lives: scary and layered, performative and striking. It all seems fake, but the money has to be real (as real as money is, in this system of loans and promises). And then there are the real feelings, which tend to get overshadowed by circular forum rhetoric. Scambaiters persist that their goal is to distract scammers, in any effective way. The Glamour Shots-style photography, then, is only a by-product of the cause, but it is clearly symptomatic of that desensitizing role that anonymity plays in encouraging extremist and base behavior. Add the vague goal of "distraction from crime," and we have permission to showcase our most unattractive urges and call them virtuous.

Hito Steyerl writes, in "Epistolary Affect and Romance Scams: Letter from an Unknown Woman" that, centuries after the first "Spanish Prisoner" scam in 1588, "this plot has been updated to resonate with contemporary wars and upheaval. Countless 419 scams... rewrite daily catastrophe as entrepreneurial plotlines. Shock capitalism and its consequences—wars over raw materials or privatization—are recast as interactive romance adventure novels...

these are 'the only forms of tragedy available to us,' as Thomas Elsaesser said about the melodrama."

Media content feels increasingly melodramatic, a response, perhaps, to the paralyzing effects of vicarious screen life. Since it is possible to exist as only an avatar of one's former self, dramatizing one's role in anonymous communications is more enticing: we are ever more inclined to amplify even the most generic of emotions. Reality shows, more than scripted dramas, cling to archaic gender roles. In them, men talk to the backs of women's crying heads and everyone ends up where they started in the end. People, especially the women, break down. "The genre of melodrama," Steyerl writes, "addresses the domestic, feminized sphere." The melodrama, she continues, "was safely kept apart from cinema-as-art for decades. It was suspected to perpetuate oppression as well as female compliance. Yet the melodrama also voiced perspectives that were repressed and forbidden."

Melodrama master Douglas Sirk said, "Melodrama is a combination of kitsch, and craziness, and trashiness... There is a very short distance between high art and trash, and trash that contains the element of craziness is by this very quality nearer to art... I am interested in circularity, in the circle—people arriving at the place they started out from. This is why you will find what I call tragic rondos in many of my films, people going in circles."

Scams of any sort rely on circular logic. They rely, too, on emotions intensifying over time. Melodrama does not simplify. It can, in fact, do the opposite. In Sirk's movies, everyone's voice seems to become louder and louder. Colors get more vivid. Remarks about the differences between men and women are made frequently. Music surges and a stag wanders through snow, a silent respite for our heroine. Unlike Sirk movies, though, modern melodramas (online-only romances, unexpected letters about espionage, etc.) are mostly interested in duplicity. Teenage sitcoms and fantasy fiction always favor the character living a double life. This mirrors our interest in becoming someone else through anonymity and foreign interaction.

Our mentality while online is undoubtedly similar to that of a melodrama's corseted and underappreciated heroine, due to the super-saturated 2-D diorama we constantly inhabit. Most of us are familiar, now, with the intense emotional spasm that comes after sending a direct message. Waiting for a reply must be just as lonely as waiting for a lover's telegram. All the circumstances have changed, meaning there are fewer excuses now to cushion a possible rejection. Melodramas involve years of waiting, but the human mind inflates loneliness, unable to fully grasp that any experience is similar to its own. Instead, we can imagine that sketches of endless waiting, impossible love, or the centuries of solitude that vampires suffer before finding someone who shares their specific miseries can come close to our feelings.

Old-fashioned courting is intrinsic to the melodrama move-ment, and so it is intrinsic to scams. Gender itself has become genre. In melodrama, much gets left out and other ingredients are doubled. The new recipe is indulgent, full of cultural differences, protective lies, and taboo. The result can end up feeling more genuine than most banal encounters of daily life. Says Steyerl, "Over-the-top exaggeration and exoticization opened possibilities to imagine something different from the drab repetitiveness of reproductive labour. Melodramas concoct implausible tales of cultural encounter, racial harmony and happiness narrowly lost in miscommunication."

The quick rise to popularity of Joanne the Scammer, a tongue-in-cheek character performed by comedian Branden Miller on multiple social media platforms proves that the act of scamming and even the aestheticizing of it as a lifestyle is intrinsic to our globalized and xenophobic present. "Caucasian" Joanne (a white female character played by a black Latino with full beard and blonde wig) endears us to the life of someone whose ultimate goal is to hustle, no matter what it be for and by what means.

Marks of scammers, too, are humanized in a proliferation of television shows on the subject. The more gullible contestants of *Catfish* and *90 Day Fiancé* are usually stuck in some small town, financially unstable, and looking for adventure through screens. They—we—are stuck on flat surfaces, trying to narrate lives as arching story plots. We crave the linearity of dramatic literature because we are conditioned for it, but the nature of networking is much more splayed than a line. It is a debate, but one with no moderator, so the arguments become more and more outrageous, until we see the grotesque and gorgeous avenues the human mind is capable of.

Scambaited drag looks elegant, even if it is scary, like moments of serenity found in war photography, the beauty of a culture heightened by its casual relationship to ugliness. The ploys in either direction are hinged on sentiment, after all. They play on sympathy for the impoverished and the orphaned, or on plain boredom. Invented stories of dying pets or the unjustly imprisoned and romantic catfishing play on a person's unmet emotions, and there are so many lonely people in this world, searching for excitement of any sort, even if it comes at a price. The act of losing oneself for the chance at a new life (a trip to America, a surplus of riches, a love connection) might be the most human impulse of them all. The fallout of a scam or scambaiting is always sticky, which is its initial allure. It reveals some essential truth about how overwhelming a promise of something better can be—how much a person will put aside for the spice of life.

The Eighties

"The campus is now divided into two groups, which refer to each other, solely on the basis of the single-sex or co-ed dormitory issue, as the lesbians and the whores... Students are 'coming out' as lesbians, who, in the old days, would have been thought of as shy, or bold, or having crushes, or simply loyal in their friend-ships, but who would not have been, probably are not now, lesbians at all. And students who are declaring themselves whores as though that were the only heterosexual choice."

— Renata Adler, *Pitch Dark*

There is this thing I love about eighties subcultures, or about the eighties in general, the way we think of the decade now, which is this particular way of compartmentalizing that seems so comfortably insincere. Since then, we've decided that subscribing to an image representative of originality is in fact presenting as unoriginal. But maybe the idea was never to be so original.

In the eighties, I imagine, to fall into a category was to feel at home somewhere, during a time when everything was abruptly commodified. We tend to imagine all of the eighties as one sharp turn towards selling out, every cliché being fed back to us, evil artists making pop sculptures and masculine paintings. But before it was so obvious that we each had to become individuals and sell that individualism as personal brands, there were stereotypes to explore, to cling to, to hide behind.

We see eras as liquid reactions, New Waves that take all of their actors with them, smoothing out all the spikes that made innovators appear outside of something, flinging them back inside of that rebellion, renaming someone "ahead of their time" as definitive of that time. The eighties created a lot of stories about types of people: pill poppers, dying gay artists, unhappy housewives. The rich play-boy, obviously: Donald Trump was a funny archetype back then. Becoming a powerful man's mistress had a little more charm, I assume.

The eighties loved fairy tales about decades past and was anxious about its own legacy. Quintessential eighties movies have a protagonist-turned-narrator, a young person talking into a camera, explaining how vapid their surroundings are, how strange it is to live in this cultural void. Genre films, in general, were bigger then: extreme action, camp horror, soapy drama, classic musical remakes, new narratives about teens discovering that it's easier to be part of some-thing than to go it alone.

Less popular were the avant-garde plotlines of the preceding eras that sometimes didn't really have plots. The surreal had become a type of kitsch. The closer one came to reality, to weird Wall Street wolves and Western actor presidents, the more improbable the story sounded.

But that's not completely right. The eighties in America was about, in so many ways, regression. The country had gone so far in the direction of new age liberal aesthetics, it had to swing back to find a balance: pastels as opposed to jewel tones; high waists as opposed to hip huggers; installations in front of corporate buildings as opposed to undocumented performances; costumed rock stars to replace those withering singer-songwriters. It was unrealistic to go on rejecting all things synthetic, including New Romantic music. Even serial murderers were products of a system the power of which we had lost control; we'd started to accept and even appreciate the monsters we'd created. The eighties, I'd say, was about vampires, in every sense.

It's bittersweet, buying into a subculture, and all subcultures have dark sides, and all of life, if you consider the amount of plastic it's made of, is bleak. The collective memory of Reagan's term is heavily made-up and hair-sprayed even at the gym, studded and pierced to the point of immobility, dancing on cocaine to the beat of a drum machine, a pop star lip-synching to an uglier person's recorded voice. Then, there was beauty in the veneer being lacquered onto everything we encountered every day: the supermarket, the criminal justice system, the art world. There was happiness in accepting, for the first time, a fully merchandized fate.

"Whores and lesbians have found an issue on which they are united…Male gyms do not have shower curtains. Male athletes are not hidden in the showers from one another. As a symptom, a residue of shame about the female body, the shower curtains, the students say, as with one voice, must be removed."

It isn't shame that the decade removed, but pretense. No one became their truer self by getting naked; they confronted a need for sexiness, competition, gender. People adhered to a characterization of themselves that was so distant from something within or about them, it was more icon than identity. Like an eighties arcade video game. What character would you have been?

Thonging

Like all studies of fashion, the thong is intrinsically connected to the history of humanity. Although the thong lies beneath the thinking behind so many historical moments, it is academically underrepresented. As goes its popularity, the thong has suffered ebbs and flows. The very form of the garment brings up anxiety: it relies on oppositional tugging to assume its preferred shape.

The origin of underwear is a disputed topic, the origin of the thong even further disputed. In the Bible, Eve's first bite into forbidden fruit summoned a fig leaf, which logically must have been tied to the wearer. In most cultures, a type of loincloth originated before a more complicated brief or bikini pattern. Anthropologically speaking, the image of the loincloth is synced with the barbarism imagined by European voyagers. Slaves and servants in Europe and in Euro-colonized countries wore loincloths to display subservience, even though the loincloth was originally a functional garment in locales where the buttocks were no more taboo a display than the legs.

The Japanese fundoshi, for example, was originally the only style of underwear worn in Japan and later became the classic garment of powerful warriors—samurais and sumo wrestlers. It is still worn by male citizens during traditional ceremonies. The fundoshi loincloth comes in a few forms, including a newer female version, and according to the *Tokyo Times*, made a comeback in the last decade as "power underwear."

Professor Otto Steinmayer says the reason behind a lack of research in the area of Eastern undergarments is the Westerner's lack of understanding of the loincloth, due to personal history. In his essay, "The Loincloth of Borneo," he refers to European men's dress as "arctic" and inherited from the Roman style of trousers and shirt. "The only thing in Europe which resembles [the loincloth] is underpants, a garment that has a history of scarcely a thousand years and whose dignity and consequent esthetic value has been nil. Europeans have always considered the loincloth an immodest garment."

This is of course because of what it leaves bare. Most cultures have at one point come up with a standardized shame concerning the nakedness of genitalia, but, Steinmayer continues, "It seems to be a peculiarly western trait to feel equal shame about the buttocks, probably from a fear of homosexuality, an anxiety which also seems to grow with civilization."

But the thong has come to represent more than primitivizing a culture's dress. A thong bathing suit has become representative of air-headed hyper-sexualization. The question of whether a feminist can wear a thong can be, according to writers Jennifer Baumgardner and Amy Richards, "a metaphor for the generation gap between older women's feminism and younger women's," in their essay, "The Number One Question about Feminism."

"At the 150 or so colleges where we have spoke since our book *Manifesta: Young Women, Feminism, and the Future* hit the shelves, the 'can I wear a thong' type of query is one of the most popular. On the surface, the statement feeds into stereotypes about young women, seeming to reveal that they are oddly obsessed with body image and shopping issues and their personal lives, rather than politics and revolution. On a different level, however, the question is symbolic of young people's relationship to feminism: meaning that the relationship is often personal, invisible, and uncomfortable."

Fashion and sex have so much in common, but the blurred lines between gender studies and fashion design sometimes make themselves clearer by drawing attention to the differing priorities on either side. It's interesting to trace skin-revealing fads and pinpoint their place in the history of radical change, for example. The birth control pill is often noted as a source for sexual revolution, bra-burning and hip huggers to follow. Underwear trends of the nineties like thick branded bands and layered boxers, arrived just after the advent of the AIDS crisis and the popularization of condom-wearing.

Someone once said to me, "a thong is like a railroad between cultural centers," meaning for bacteria, an image I can't forget. A cheap thong looks like something that has washed ashore and dried out, but a nicer thong is sexy, suggestive, even endearing. The wearing of the thong can mean a multitude of deviant actions. It is strangely at once conservative and reactionary. Consider the conundrum of hiding panty lines by creating the illusion of underwearlessness.

In the nineties, a new wave of thong popularity and mass-acceptance was ushered in by a mainstream linguistic shift. In 1992, MTV played Kyuss's grungey "Thong Song," which contained the lyrics, "My hair's real long/no brains, all groin/no shoes, just thongs/I hate slow songs." In 1999, this title was already dated enough to allow a new song with the same name to play on MTV and become a huge success. Kyuss's understanding of the word as a type of footwear was now laughable, while Sisqó's was the agreed-upon definition. Comparing the two videos provides not only an illustration of the changing definition of the word "thong," but of the changing expectations of music videos on MTV.

Sisqó's and Dru Hill's "Thong Song" was regarded as a danceable summer joke, but its video was typical of R&B seducers of its time in terms of high production value, dramatic structure, and objectifying women. 1999 was also the year Juvenile's "Back That Azz Up" came out. In my staticky memory, the video for the radio-friendly version, "Back That Thang Up," became the most requested video on my local network TV's experimental all-request channel, The Box. This video's devoted low-budget look depicted a block party, not a beach party, and inspired a generation of sexually explicit rap content. Instead of designer bathing suits and rooftop pools, the women in this video dress casually and dance in streets or front yards. The extreme slow motion of "Back That Thang Up" made it clear that these women were wearing either nothing or a thong under their thin denim and khaki shorts, thereby making this video more sexual in nature than Sisqó's, which mostly showed boy-cut bathing suits.

Three of the most notable aftereffects of "Back That Thang Up" are Nelly's 2003 remix "Tip Drill," Ludacris's 2007 single, "P-Poppin'," and Sisqó's 2000 sequel to "Thong Song." In the video for the new version of "Thong Song" (created for the soundtrack to *The Nutty Professor II: The Klumps*), a change has occurred: Dancers are wearing thongs. The slow motion ass-take is repeated and the focus has changed from a glance at a group of partying girls to a long stare at each girl's thong, one at a time. The video still has a narrative, but more attention is placed on texture.

The (censored) video to "Tip Drill"—the chorus of which goes, "It must be that ass, cuz it ain't your face"—uses a similar style of cinematography, taking the theme of voyeuristic intrusion one step further. It speaks of and shows women wearing thongs and taking them off, whereas "Thong Song" only asks someone to show the thong itself. "P-Poppin'" became "Booty Poppin'" for MTV. The video, which tells the story of a dance contest at the notorious Magic City strip club in Atlanta, got limited air-time. The TV-friendly video is so blurred it was essentially an advertisement for the director's cut that could be found online.

In videos that spare no sensitivity to subject, camera-light is infrequently directed at female faces, instead focusing on the literal pulling of G-strings. Women in "Tip Drill" and "Booty Poppin'" are stripping in a club, competing for a famous rapper's attention in his home, or table dancing at a sweaty party, their undergarments stretching and breaking.

The thong, like these artistic depictions, is marginalized. It is a hidden object, squeezed between lobes, becoming obscure (unable to fight the battle of visibility because of the very position that defines it), and therefore misunderstood. It denotes sexual deviance while it suggests an understanding of realness. The thong is centimeters closer to areas of arousal, which means it is that much closer to the truth. It is at once decorative and invisible, like the selling of sex itself. It asks what sex would feel like without censorship, what pornography would look like without an underground industry, and how far one can be pulled in any direction.

Celebrity

Confidence

The first time I met Ally, I kissed her. I'd been asked by the designers of Eckhaus Latta to act in their *Friends* opening sequence-inspired fashion film, and I was to play Ally's girlfriend. We were setting up the shot in a tiny Chinatown apartment and she arrived late, announcing that she'd been having lunch with her sugar daddy. He had just bought her a pair of pink Ugg boots. She should have just asked for the money, she said, but she really wanted the Uggs. She had just spontaneously quit a paid internship at Calvin Klein to focus on her art and dancing. Mike Eckhaus and Zoe Latta explained the scene to her and introduced me. Ally seemed tired, like this was just another day's work. After all, her life was hinged on false intimacy, and performative kissing was what she did to pay the bills.

Ally—or some combination of "artist," "arttits" "artburp," "thot-catalog," "artwerk," and the repeated number six—had taken selfie-ing to a new level as part of her art practice, creating uncomfortably inward-looking portraits, when I was asked to interview her.

"I've definitely gotten critiques like, 'What are you showing that's new here?'" she told me of the nudes that frequently resulted in her social media profiles being deleted or suspended for content violations. "Selfies are a generational phenomenon that I've gotten really good at. Now it's at a point where my selfies are taken for entirely different reasons than they used to be. I find myself doing it less and less. And that's partly informed by my feeling that my image doesn't make enough impact. I'm still just a skinny white person."

The fact that Ally's features are, as some have observed, "perfect," give her images more poignancy than if she was not classically beautiful, for better or worse. A social-media Venus de Milo in varyingly sexy and ungainly poses, Ally's art explores the ambivalence underlying a generation's selfie obsession. We cannot look away, and yet we want to fix what we're looking at: smooth it over, or straighten it out. An imagined perfection seems to hover tantalizingly within reach, pulling our yearning tighter until it becomes a confusing, sexualized emotion akin to the feelings inspired by pornography. Looking at Ally's images is like looking at something too expensive to buy, or feeling jealous of art you know you could have made. But look closer: Ally is always staring at herself as intently as you are, and she feels the same way.

"I had thousands of friends on Snapchat," she told me. "A lot of them were underage girls sending me nudes, being like, 'You make me feel good about my body.' I was being such an exhibitionist, and receiving their pictures and responding to them made them feel comfortable. I don't know if it's because I have a good body or because it's a naked body being put out there by a personality they find interesting. Then again, I've had friends tell me they've unfollowed me because they don't like seeing pictures of me naked. It makes them mad or gives them body dysmorphia. That sucks."

Ally was no longer on Snapchat, and on Instagram, her beautified, backstage model shots were being replaced by pictures taken exclusively at home. In fact, she said, she didn't leave her apartment often. When I buzzed Ally outside her Brooklyn building, a disembodied voice sang, "Come up, come into my house," and the door unlocked. I was surprised to see small chandeliers and fake marble in the stairwell, and even more surprised when Ally's boyfriend, Jasper, and his puppy led me up to the fourth floor apartment. It looked like a dance studio. Roommate and model Michael Bailey Gates walked by and waved. Some guests on the couch were preparing to leave. Ally greeted me in a flesh-colored bra and panty set under a sheer dress and green knee socks.

She led me to her bedroom, which looked like a fabric store, with spooled clothing stacked on open shelves: hyper-organized chaos. Dozens of scarves and hundreds of necklaces hung from pegs above her bed. Another shelf was filled with piles of platform pumps.

That Ally was able to be in this beautiful space almost all day, every day put an elephant in the room. She still had the sugar daddy, she confirmed, before stressing: "I am financially independent, and I have tons of friends who aren't. Who doesn't? That's New York, right?"

She considered dates with her sugar daddy sex work, although no sex was involved. She described their relationship as that of therapist and patient, but, although she was making the money, she was also the one being counseled. "I talk to him about my shit and he tells me the few things in the world he can't tell his wife." Before I could ask, she said that her boyfriend wasn't happy about this arrangement. To her credit, the transparency with which she spoke was refreshingly rare. It's almost common knowledge that incomes like this one, only secreted away, are what make the New York art world turn.

"He wants to have sex, obviously," she added, afraid I might think her naïve. "Why would he still be paying me to hang out with him? He's asked me a million times. He's offered me enough money that it would make sense to do it, but I don't. I used to dance for him, years ago. He's almost like a patron, in a weird way. I really care about him. I love him, I do. But to be honest, and this is terrible in a way, I think I would be fine without him as a source of income."

She said she was getting enough money from modeling work. Ally studied fashion at Rhode Island School of Design, commuting from her "starving artist" mother's house nearby. She described her father as a businessman in Hong Kong. The summer after her junior year, she interned in New York while dancing at an exclusive gentlemen's party. She moved to the city after school, taking internships at DIS and VFILES, where she met Hari Nef, who was attending Columbia and performing in a drag troupe called Chez Deep. Later, Hari became the first transgender model to sign with IMG and eventually started acting in films and television. A few years back, though, Hari wasn't at all sure what she wanted to do for work. She and a boyfriend had moved into two of the rooms in Ally's apartment.

I asked Hari what she was like back then. "When I met Ally, she was working as an exotic dancer. I remember when she told me, casually after work one day. At that point she had also worked with the design team at Calvin Klein. She talked about the various aspects of her work as if they comprised a gradient. I was still a teenager when we met, fresh from the suburbs, so I hadn't met very many sex—or sexy—workers in my life. She owned that aspect of her work. It was another creative endeavor. She changed the way I looked at sex, then work, then sex work. I was electrified by the idea that she included exotic dancing as part of her practice, not just a side gig to pay the bills. I view her work as a gesture of militant self-love, aggressive body positivity, sad girl catharsis, a parochialization of the ideal female body. I think she's kind of a hero, proof that punk is alive and well. She was one of the people I met in New York whose work helped me to feel okay about being myself."

If she could do anything forever, Ally would do everything she's already doing. "I don't even want to design clothes, really," she said, lying back on her bed with a cigarette, gesturing towards a closet that apparently held collected garments intended for a design project.

"The thing is, I'd do any of these things if I had to, but if I can get away with doing whatever the fuck I want, I'm gonna do that instead. I want to be an artist. That's a vague term and I use it because I want to do a lot of different things within that umbrella. It's coming slowly. I do do a lot of things. I've been conceptualizing a solo show for a long time that needs to happen. It doesn't need to happen at all, actually. But it would be cool if it did, because I've talked about it enough."

The concept behind this solo show would rely on the very idea that someone like Ally having a solo show in New York City doesn't quite make sense. "Ultimately, in the contemporary art industry, you follow a pattern: you follow certain steps, you climb a certain ladder. I would basically just be skipping a bunch of steps." She has made drawings, some of which are scribbles on prints of her mother's oil paintings. And she has cried, heavy make-up leaking down her face, in a performance with her friend Petra Collins at Art Basel in Miami Beach.

The collaboration that generated the most heat perhaps is a set of images Richard Prince made of her. They're not the infamous Instagram frames from his "New Portraits" series, but the artists did meet through Instagram, as did, tangentially, Ally and photographer Mario Sorrenti, who shot her with her friends in a CK One campaign referencing his own nineties Kate Moss Obsession ads. Mario is "a sweetie," she said. Richard, on the other hand, is "a really great bad guy," who came to her apartment and talked for two hours before he shot her for ten minutes.

"I was a big fan of his before I became this, like, anarchist feminist artist type. I like him, because I think appropriation in general is fascinating and amazing, and it's happening constantly. Some people are obvious about it and some are more stealthy, but it's everywhere. Richard Prince gets away with murder because he does it really well. Do I think he's a good person in general? I don't know, not really. I don't think he would say that he is."

Ally showed me the resulting prints on her phone: black-and-white nudes collaged with aggressive line drawings that cover her face. Richard sent her a canvas printed with one of her own Instagram images, she mentions, but it may never have shown anywhere. Underground art pornographer Richard Kern, too, shot Ally in this apartment.

"We've talked a lot about Richard Prince together," Ally laughed when I asked her about Kern. "Richard Prince appropriated a ton of Richard's photos when they were younger. Kern said Prince was cool to him the way he was cool to me. He charms you and then he kind of uses you and drops you and it's like, whatevs."

We talked about how modeling jobs often asked Ally to shave her body hair, but she refused. Miley Cyrus had just started growing out her armpit hair then. "I had a dream about Miley once," Ally said. "The night before, I'd had a dream about Rihanna. We were in a club and Rihanna ended up being mean to me because I think we were wearing pants that looked similar and mine were way better or something. It was stupid. But then the next night, Miley took me into this dope-ass house in LA and she was just really fucking cool, really chill. We smoked weed and got along really well."

Maybe this was the story: like Miley and her stoned, goofy-faced and zit-creamed Instagram account, Ally reached a young audience afraid of its own shallowness, but from closer to home. "I don't try to make myself appear significantly cooler than I actually am, if that makes sense. Like, I'm a cool person, you're a cool person, I know a lot of fucking cool people. I'm jealous of everyone all the time, it's terrible. Instagram doesn't make it easier. But I try to be like, 'Look, I broke out or I'm PMS-ing or I'm in bed and smoking cigarettes again.' These things happen. There are plenty of people whose Instagrams I find it hard to relate to."

Ally's rejection of the celebrity and art worlds she's navigated with such ease is part of what attracted artists to her. There's something alluring about how un-aspirational her images are. Her photos were about the same things as everyone else's—comfort, food, friends, new underwear—but there was a messy self-awareness that would make them more interesting than any other hot girl's on your feed, at least for some time, before others started doing the same thing.

Unlike most models, Ally used her Instagram as a gallery, not a calling card. Her body of work, which was most easily represented by her own physical body, explored the ways that people—from uptight teenage girls to salivating older men—experienced desire. Where does the insecurity stop and the sexual attraction start? If you were completely satisfied with your own body, would you feel any less anxious? Is cataloguing that body—or any body—inherently narcissistic?

"She's an artist, yes," said Hari, to the question of what catchall best described Ally. "And she's a model, for sure. But I think she is too active and opinionated to be a muse. Ally is not malleable. She inspires people. She's not sitting on anybody's stool."

Aspiration

If only Krystal were awaiting a prisoner of war, a letter from a sailor, news of the survivors of a natural disaster. If only she could see him clearly, hovering like nebulous clouds on the planetarium's domed ceiling, everything except for his face, which would be a blank flesh color compared to his clothing, his stance, and his uncalculated movements. If only she were waiting for him, watching him walking in slow motion, and suspended in hanging shadows, a person except for that unrecognizable face, because, she'd heard, if you can't remember what a person's face looks like, it means you feel something for them.

Poor little rich girl could not aptly describe her. Her parents probably had a lot of money, but she didn't know where they put it. Stuck in suburbia wouldn't aptly describe her situation. She didn't live directly downtown, but she wasn't that far away. She was not living on a farm, tumbling down hills of Lawrencian temptations, throwing herself at the land for desperation of escaping it. She was not holed up in her parents' apartment, awaiting cease-fire or a tin can phone call. She was not even in an apartment at all, and neither one of her parents were dead; they weren't even divorced. She went to a school, not private, not in a ghetto, not even specializing in music or technology or airplane flying.

She had friends, and some of them were mean, but others were not, and they all slept over at her house because her parents had good snacks and a bedroom far away from the TV in the family room. The family room was lower in elevation than the rest of the house; it had a carpeted step leading down to it. When the sleeping bags were laid out on the ground, her mother said they looked like a bunch of noodles in a bowl; she called them "girl soup."

She didn't live in a modern condo or a "loft space" or an ocean-front house that could be blown away or vandalized by surfers that were jealous of their property. She didn't even live by an ocean. No great expanse of water crashed into itself anywhere near her; she could not go throwing herself at that, either. She couldn't even ride her bike out to look at a big lake and wonder about its bottom, or fish for hours and days until someone came by to teach her what she was doing wrong. She didn't even have a bike. And that was because they lived on an incline, and her father was worried she would break something even learning how to ride with training wheels. So she didn't know how to ride a bike, or fish, or even swim, and yet she was not one of those hopeless, soft girls who could fall easily into pockets of school that offered solace for hopelessness and softness: witchcraft, recreational prescription drugs and other types of mutual masturbation. She played a few sports. She was not the best and not the worst.

No, she was not a virgin, which would maybe be something remarkable. No she was not an only child, although she felt like one, if someone could feel such a thing. No, she had not moved many times, and she had not lived in this house her entire life either. She'd only lived there for as long as she could remember.

Her country was at war now, and nothing had changed. The TV was on almost twenty-four hours a day for about five days, and then it was back to normal. She didn't know any firemen, world-traders, government officials or soldiers. America was like a canvas, stretched to its limit, all of the tension at its edges. If she were in California, she would be on the edge of excess. If she were in New York, she would feel the collective resentment of the world and think it ordinary. Near Canada was ice and near Mexico was gunfire. Florida was capsizable, on the edge of Columbia and ugly wealth, and the rest of the south was so stark and hot some people turned into animals. The middle was tight like a drum, she imagined: If she was right in the middle of America, she would suffer, she would be stuck like a fly in a spider's web, she would feel pain from movement, either her own, or from the reverberations of what happened in Washington and on those deadly coasts, as seen on TV.

But she wasn't even stuck. Her parents were offering to pay for college tuition next year, and they were telling her to apply everywhere. They would pay for the applications, and they'd go with her for visits if the schools were within driving distance. But what if she did go to New York, or LA? What if someone in San Francisco found her wandering away from campus, brought her to his shabby bedroom and, while lighting a joint and pouring real-life dandelion wine, asked, "So, what's your deal?" What would she say? She thought about lying and starting over, but had no reason to do that. What was her deal? She didn't know.

"We're going to Big O's," Frankie said to Krystal on the phone. "They're holding auditions for *The Real World.*'"

"You want to be on *The Real World*?"

"Yeah, why not? I'm gonna be the ex-Mormon. They've never had one of those."

A year later, Krystal was pretty sure that the reason she'd been picked was not her normalcy. Another girl, Ginger, was way more normal: raised Protestant but only went to church on holidays, had only one boyfriend and basically planned on marrying him (before she was on the show).

Krystal moved to New York after filming. It was far easier than she'd thought it would be. Someone from the show met her at the airport and she had her things sent. She had three new roommates. A girl she'd met at a premiere party in LA who was a student at NYU invited her to live with her and a PR person and a PA to some gallery owner. Krystal got a job at a different gallery in Chelsea and hung out eating baklava from the bodega across the street and smoking cigarettes under the brick-red awning.

Sometimes her mom would ask her things like, "But what are you trying to be? What are you doing out there?" and Krystal would answer the only way she now knew how, based on all those conversations, all those nights in the city, at one of ten bars on the LES. "It doesn't matter these days, mom. There aren't as many titles; it's just, making it. No one's an aspiring actress, or an aspiring model, or an aspiring writer. They're just aspiring, or not aspiring, or having had aspired, and now are."

She got a boyfriend, and he was rich and famous. She didn't know who he was before she met him, which he thought was charming. He had known who she was, and she knew it was better that way. "That wasn't the real me, though, on the show."

"Of course it wasn't, or they wouldn't call it *The Real World*."

He was one of the people that told her not to doom herself with a category. They were sometimes photographed together. Maybe it was because the photographers recognized him, or maybe they knew her, but why would that matter, they said. It did matter. Like one cockroach in the silverware drawer, it was a sign of a bigger problem.

When they went back to his apartment in SoHo he would say things like, "My bed" or, "my bathroom," when he could have said, "the bed" and "the bathroom." When they fell asleep, he slowly moved his arm back out from under hers and turned onto his other side. His hands would gently cup his genitals. She slept there more often than she slept at home because she lived with roommates in an inconvenient part of Brooklyn, and he was alone and close in Manhattan.

Visiting home, Krystal said to Frankie, "I almost wish I'd never left." She looked at the swings behind her parents' house and longed to sit on one, but didn't. She saw the ceiling fan whip around so quickly she could only see the blades on every other turn they made. She could never explain her new life to Frankie, who was better off for not getting a part on the show, but also stupid for staying here, getting a job at a fucking gas station.

The ceiling fan came loose, flew towards them, sliced off their heads and neatly cut them into ribbons, despite the dullness of the veneered wood. Krystal's boyfriend sent her vague text messages that she both wanted to respond to, wittily, and to ignore. She really liked him. She wanted things to work out. She wanted things to be better in New York. She wanted to feel cleaner, and to not wake up tired, and to love walking everywhere.

A cloud moved over the house and the shadow thickened the glass of the window. In a few years she'd done almost every drug out there, felt the urgencies and lazinesses and soiled plans and showers of honest, pure light brought on by each. She'd become a tiny rodent in a crowd of millions, burrowing through tunnels quicker than the trains could take her. She felt an inexplicable loss when she realized that the thing that most bothered her boyfriend about her personality was something she could never get rid of.

"I still don't know why they picked me," Krystal said.

"You were sort of the hot nerd."

"What do people think of me now?"

"You're the girl that was on *The Real World*." Frankie put on a radio announcer voice. "What do you think your former self would think if she knew this would be you?"

Krystal put on a Hollywood girl-next-door voice. "Oh my god, I have no idea." She floated back in time and said, If only I'd known. She floated back in time and cut her wrists in a bathtub, looking perfect. But I did know, she said. Her phone vibrated softly and she put a hand in her pocket. She felt a pill she'd forgotten about and held it, and she was still, and quiet, and happy. The ceiling fan spun as Frankie tried to think of more to say. The chains of the swings would feel oily beneath their hands. Krystal tried to see her boyfriend's face and could only picture the photographs she'd seen in magazines.

"As far as the Kardashian circle, I think we're a lot more different than we are similar," says twenty-three-year-old Brooklyn native Amina Blue. It's a comparison that she has heard many times, for a few reasons. Although Blue isn't the child of a modern-day stage mom growing up in California, it's hard to find a surface-level factoid about her that couldn't also be said of a Kardashian or a Jenner. Except: "I'm vegan, and they're kind of heavy on the fur and animal products," she points out. "We just work together. We work really well together. We get stuff done." She pauses and then adds, "I guess you can't really judge until you're fully in their shoes. They have a lot to deal with."

An "it girl" can define her era, and the twenty-teens are somewhat defined by privacy and the attempt to protect it. In the nineties, "it girl" could refer to someone who was more recognized for her personality than for her career—that is, someone whose personal life or rapport with the press tended to overshadow her work. Still, she usually worked, becoming a media darling only by way of projects that needed attention. Reality television changed that, and then social media changed it again.

Today, the term has come to stand in for a word not yet invented, one that loosely means "famous first" (or, that phrase made popular in the early days of *Keeping up with the Kardashians*, "famous for being famous"). Perhaps the girl described as "it" today doesn't have any projects she wants to share. It could be that she's not very personable with the press, either, and that instead she communicates directly with her fans from home. Possibly, she became "it" before she even knew exactly what she wanted to be.

Blue's relative fame came faster than anyone could have anticipated, by way of the most exalted family on social media. She's a music video vixen, most prominently featured in Tyga's "1 of 1," filmed while the rapper was on a break with then-girlfriend Kylie Jenner. She's a model, too, best known for removing a pair of stiletto mules during the infamously uncomfortable Yeezy Season 4 fashion show. It was Kanye West who introduced her to stylist and magazine editor Carine Roitfeld, who promptly invited her to the annual New York Fashion Week party Harper's Bazaar Icons. Blue attended in a black satin dress with which undergarments of any kind would be impossible to hide.

Blue was photographed by Mert & Marcus in a shoot art-directed by West at his Calabasas home starring West's wife Kim, Kim's sister Khloé, and a handful of other celebrities. Even next to the two Kardashians, Blue's curves look surreal. West did the story for *032c*, and where the German magazine could have had a Kardashian coup for a cover, they instead went with a cropped nude Blue.

West took to Blue during a Busta Rhymes video shoot in which Blue was an extra, and cast her in every Yeezy project since. She calls him a mentor and friend. Plus, she says, he has more influence over her generation than anyone. "I've seen people go crazy for this man. His followers are so dedicated and so sincere." She adds, "The thing with Kanye is that I don't think he plays many games. Everything that comes out of his mouth is usually what he's thinking. You just gotta take what he says and deal with it. I know a lot of people are upset with that whole Trump thing. I was, too, like: What's he doing with Trump? But once you hear his reasoning—and I'm not saying

I agree with it—you know, everybody's different. Maybe it's a good thing that he's meeting the president of the United States. If you can't beat 'em you might as well just join 'em."

Named for her icy eyes, Blue views every person she meets as an opportunity to learn, she tells me. West's in-laws give plenty of lessons on "what to do and what not to do." But reality television isn't, according to Blue, what not to do. In fact, she's shot a pilot for VH1 that follows her and other "influencers" (a title she prefers).

The world of celebrity changes daily. Picture the nineties: A Page Six reporter befriends a cool girl at a party, agreeing to scratch her back if she'll make a good story. Back then, when fashion preferred relatively miniscule butts, political correctness and the internet were relatively new concepts. Fame was both less stigmatized and less accessible—an "it girl" had to go out, be seen, and be charming.

By comparison, "it girls" of today will most likely have been discovered via social media. Their art direction, more than anything else, gets them through doors. They are, more often than not, self-described homebodies, even antisocial. Today, a cool girl is coaxed from a bedroom iPhone shoot into a professional studio. Blue describes herself, like so many of today's overnight influencers do, as "pretty boring." Her image could at once represent her generation's particular acceptance of overexposure and its acute discomfort with pressure to perform.

Blue's evasiveness, for example, seems to fan the emotional flames of her similarly aged followers. After the world was privy to the striking features on display at Yeezy's first fashion show, Blue was made a voiceless meme. Kylie Jenner modeled in the same show, barely recognizable in a wig cap and oversized blazer, while Blue looked like a cross between Storm and Betty Boop as painted by Mark Ryden, in little more than a transparent bodysuit.

Almost every public move Blue made, once she went viral, was steeped in controversy. "I get people writing to me from Kylie's fan pages," Blue says, "and they are the most threatening and rude and obnoxious comments. They'll argue with my regular fans. Most of the comments I get are really positive, asking me how to eat better and be vegan." Anyway, she laughs, "All press is good press."

The negativity started after Tyga posted behind-the-scenes snaps of his "1 of 1" video on Snapchat, the camera giving Blue elevator eyes before she coyly parts a white robe to reveal a tattooed hip. On top of the side chick BTS suggestion, the video itself cast her, a bleached-blonde woman of German-Pakistani descent, as a Jamaican (it's not just the cornrows—the dialogue drives this narrative home).

Find one of the many videos of the five-foot one-inch Blue walking stiffly down an outdoor runway on New York's Roosevelt Island before removing her sweaty plastic Yeezy heels and you'll find comments picking her and others apart for not being "real models." Even before the shoes came off, Season 4's open casting call was published, requesting "multi-racial women only," which started a turbulent conversation online about stigmatizing and diluting blackness.

Perhaps another indicator that Blue could encapsulate her generation's dismorphic aspirations is that she is pale in complexion with bigger lips and hips than most white women. She's inadvertently the unnamed and politically incorrect ideal. The youngest Jenner sister has put up with similar accusations of race-appropriation that stem from her admitted use of injections and hair extensions. But, "I don't really talk to Kylie," Blue confirms. "She's not one of the Kardashians I'm friends with."

Perhaps another reason why internet-age "it girls" like Blue are such homebodies is the potential trauma that comes with exponential growth of attention. Blue doesn't seem phased by an excess of aggression directed at her, but she's likely good at masking her emotions.

Since she turned eighteen, she's been getting tattooed, despite wanting to work as a model. Large figures crawl up a thigh and around a shoulder. On her chest is an Eye of Horus that at least one Kanye hater has publicly described as a symbol of the Illuminati.

Blue lives with four pit bulls because she couldn't find homes for three of her dog's thirteen puppies. She recently bought a house to renovate in North Carolina, where her grandmother lives, for when she wants "a change" from Brooklyn life. "If I don't have to go outside, I'd rather not," she says. "I'm not a party person. I don't go to the club often. I have a really weak stomach and I throw up everywhere. I'll have a glass of wine, but with hard liquor I can't do it."

The aversion to alcohol has made being involved in rap video shoots less of a draw. She doesn't do much of that anymore. "I did some bottle service at a strip club and honestly that was enough for me," she says. "There was some crazy shit in there. I enjoyed it and the money was great, but I did it for a little bit and now I'm done."

A major influence for Blue is actress, model, and fellow vegan shoe designer Pamela Anderson. "She has a bubbly personality," which is something Blue admires, having discovered in the strip club that she couldn't be as cunning in business as the dancers were. "I can be friendly, but in that type of environment it's hard to be friendly." Being able to be friendly in every type of environment is the goal, she adds. "I saw that the most successful people were the ones that could have a conversation with anybody about anything. That's what made them stand out." In other words, Blue wants to be the type of person who can make it look like she actually likes leaving the house, apparently oblivious that at this point, she'd get more jobs if she stayed home.

Legacy

"Coco?"

A girl in a delicate silk shirt looked up shyly from her seat at a crowded coffee chain. We'd spoken on the phone a few days ago, and I guessed she wasn't the type to jump up and air kiss. Instead, she half-smiled and lowered her sparkling, solemn eyes. She looked a perfect composite of her well-known parents, as if she had gotten to pick the more rounded nose, fuller lips, blonder hair and longer legs. She wasn't a model, yet. She had no agency and no publicist. Her school email address was listed on her website, which featured her latest drawings and paintings: stark, sometimes funny multimedia efforts that sort of perfectly sum up the deep despondency of the average millennial—and of the college-age kid suffering the first crushing realities that come with leaving home. In the coffee shop, nobody recognized her.

In fact, up until earlier that year, very little was publicly known about Coco Hayley Gordon Moore, the daughter of Kim Gordon and Thurston Moore, founding members of the unparalleled indie influence that was Sonic Youth. A quick Google search brought up only the record of a regular girl's coming of age: braces-filled Myspace-era snapshots and childhood birthday parties. All of that changed in July of 2015, when Marc Jacobs chose some of his best friends and biggest inspirations to model in his Fall/Winter campaign. Kim and Coco simply had to pose: Kim, after all, was in the first-ever Marc

Jacobs ad. Later, in 2003, another campaign featured her again, this time with her family: husband Thurston, a niece, and daughter Coco.

One would expect Coco to be an all-around "it girl" by the time of our interview, whether she wanted it or not, but so far she'd somehow fended it off. It was just one of the traits that made her, in my eyes, the ultimate millennial in terms of attitude. Hers may be the first generation that doesn't want to be famous, since being well known now means being picked apart. "My Instagram is private," she said. "I'm a pretty private person in general." I asked if she'd met many other celebrities' kids to compare herself to. "Oh yeah," she smiled. "Totally different points of view. I remember meeting some who acted much more grown up than me, already drinking and smoking. That was not me; I was a late bloomer, or maybe normal, but late in that context."

She'd just finished posing for a *Dazed* cover shoot with Collier Schorr, who is represented by 303 Gallery, Kim's New York gallery. Schorr's involvement in the shoot was what caught the attention of the normally camera-shy twenty-one-year-old. Although "shy" isn't quite the right word. Coco is quietly confident in person, yet surprisingly age-appropriate in her mannerisms, with an un-flirty practicality not often seen in girls her age this pretty.

"I've seen first-hand what fame can do to a person, and I have no interest in it." It's not quite hypocritical. This story most likely won't make her any more famous than she already is—even if, up until now, she hadn't done a single print interview or posed for a studio portrait alone. Fame is relative. But with recent developments in her family, the demand for access to her life increased. And if she was going to be seen, Coco wanted some control over how. She had lived in the Midwest and attended the School of the Art Institute in Chicago since 2011, the year she left her Northampton, Massachusetts home, and the year that her parents and their band broke up. Before we met, she sent me a link to the website she made at school to display her artwork. It featured a selfie in which her face was obscured.

Looking at a printout of one of her newer paintings, which repeats a scrawled phrase she's used in at least one other work, "Today I broke a chair," she explained, "I like that it has a lot of different meanings. It can be that someone sat down and it was accidental, or that it was in anger." A series called "Gossip Paintings" uses overheard fragments of conversation and inside jokes to make an otherwise stark composition much friendlier. Not surprisingly, she said she was influenced by Raymond Pettibon's work—which happens to include an iconic sleeve for Sonic Youth's 1990 album, *Goo*.

Perhaps because she was in awe of her family circle's cultural influence, Coco's eyes were always ready to roll in reverence. "Growing up, every time I'd bring something to my parents, they'd be like, 'Yeah, we know,' or, 'Yeah, you met him as a baby.'" Even when she spoke of other things—like friends, boys, and pop music—Coco didn't dissolve into nervous giggles. Her voice is a slightly higher-pitched version of her mother's notorious monotone. Other similarities between herself and Kim that Coco ended up naming are their "aesthetics, conceptual interests," and fashion senses. She and her close cousins "wear a lot of X-Girl," the brand Kim co-founded in 1993. "We love it."

I asked about their shared music tastes, and Coco finally laughed. "I like pretty much everything she likes, but she does not like a lot of the music I do, like pop radio. The stuff I listened to when I was younger, she hated. My dad didn't care. He would try and get into it."

Coco's now defunct Tumblr revealed even more of what the trio do and don't have in common, as it was filled with images from the nineties, including a young Gwen Stefani and *Poison Ivy*-era Drew Barrymore, but there were plenty of Drake gifs, too. Also, a crowd shot from the *Simpsons* episode in which Sonic Youth guest star. In 2011, she had to face the pitfalls of online exposure head-on, and started deleting.

"It was a hard year," she sighed. "Dealing with the internet when that was happening was hard, because everyone knew. People were taking sides when they didn't know what was happening. Parents getting a divorce is hard for any kid, but it was also icons separating, because I can't help but view them like that."

When her parents and their band split up, a sect of Gen X felt as if their parents were divorcing, too. In some ways, it was worse: any average person's parents might easily be broken up by something as clichéd as a younger woman. The average person's parents weren't a power couple, or as cultured and influential as Kim Gordon and Thurston Moore. It's another way in which Coco's ultimate millennial status comes together, but also falls apart. Like an apprehensive social media influencer, her suffering is everyone's, but worse. She'd rather keep it to herself, though.

Next, Kim's memoir, *Girl in a Band*, became the exemplary last word on a couple that seemed unbreakable. "I've read parts of it," said Coco, "but I can't read the whole thing. It gets really emotional for me." Since the divorce, Kim moved to Los Angeles, where her daughter visits her. Thurston moved to London ("I think," said Coco), where she didn't plan on visiting. "It's too long on a plane," she added, referencing a recently developed fear of flying. In 2011, Licorice, the cat whose name Coco has tattooed on her wrist, also disappeared.

The refocused spotlight on her family clearly made Coco more aware of her online perception. "I do think about it maybe more than other people, because it's going to be referenced as, 'This is their daughter and this is what she's doing.' I guess people do look up my name, and that's horrifying. I don't think about it that much until someone sends me a link that's like, 'People are talking about this.' Someone made me a Wikipedia page and my parents had it taken down because it was so creepy. It said I was in a band in fourth grade. Like, how do you know that?"

On politics: "People expect me to be really feminist because my mom is such a feminist icon. It's a subject I've stayed away from, or tried to not say too much about, just because it's complicated and there are so many views on what it is and what we should do about it." Her beliefs seemed inoffensive enough—"equal rights and equal pay," she explained in one breath—but she'd seen what making statements less bold can do to a well-meaning woman. Instead, she jokes. Her Twitter feed (@mooreweed) proffers remarks that gain an extra edge knowing where they come from, such as "a guy just said 2 me 'whats up slut, dirty whore'. i would have said something if i wasn't in such a rush to get to chipotle!"

In another of Coco's paintings I read the phrase, "Today I spent 14 hours in my room on my computer." As per her instruction, I considered different readings of the statement. Here's one: according to the contemporary narrative, rich histories are finally available at our fingertips, thanks to the internet. But none of it is truly within reach. Sonic Youth is one such history that none of us, not even the direct offspring of it, can live. The nineties, as seen by millennials, were the last decade of ignorant bliss. The youth of that era made the stoner their totemic figure of cool, whereas the "it attitude" of today is closer to a well-researched paranoiac. I asked Coco if she, too, ever considered that she was perhaps the quintessential millennial, and instead of giving me a quote to be taken out of context, she slowly nodded.

The Drop

Insomniac, founded by Pasquale Rotella in 1993, is a production company that puts on some of the biggest parties in the world, with hundreds of thousands of attendees. After a reported legal scare involving allegations of embezzlement, conspiracy, and bribery in 2012 and many drug-related deaths occurring at Insomniac's Electric Daisy Carnivals worldwide, Rotella has become versed in deflecting scrutiny during interviews. For example, he often brings up the wonder of a child, his child, Rainbow Aurora Rotella, and how the toddler inspired in him to create atmospheres that evoke childlike wonder in adults.

"Becoming a father has been the most amazing chapter of my life," Rotella told me, just as he has told hundreds of writers. "Every day is a new adventure. First words, first steps, birthday parties…" He brought Rainbow, in 2013, to her first EDC at three months old. When I asked about his rise to EDM hero status, another canned response: "The culture is so much bigger than one person, but I definitely believe we all need to play our part and come to the table with a positive attitude."

If you follow Rotella, his wife, former Playboy Playmate and *The Girls Next Door* star Holly Madison, or Insomniac on social media, you've likely seen Rainbow. You may have even seen blown-up photos of the child being held above crowds on homemade totems. As the famous couple and their millions of fans have pointed out, their daughter, who is still too young to truly experience EDC, has become a symbol of its intentions—mainly Positive Vibes (#FollowTheRainbow).

Rave culture has always valorized extremes and contradictions: in the nineties, the mantra PLUR (peace, love, unity, respect) would show up written in beads on backpacks full of contraband and on the bracelets of minors passed out against port-a-potties, bright lights and smiley faces decorating what were essentially unsupervised carnival haunted houses.

EDC New York is actually held in New Jersey's MetLife Stadium. A competing New York EDM festival, Electric Zoo, takes place on Randall's Island, Manhattan. The year I went to both, 2013, the third day of EZoo was cancelled due to two deaths and at least four other MDMA-related hospitalizations. The two fatalities, a twenty-three-year-old man and a twenty-year-old woman who were rushed off the island that night, had travelled from Rochester, New York, and Providence, Rhode Island, respectively. Vocally outraged ticket holders for that final day were refunded for their nearly two-hundred-dollar tickets. The city of New York shut down the event to make sure no one else was hurt, but to be clear, putting a stop to a cash flow of this scale is the rarity, not the deaths of the excited, overheated young adults. In fact, a death or two happens at a handful of other music festivals every year.

"There's the temperature problems, there's drug abuse problems, there's a massive amount of people," Leighton James of the Canadian dub step duo Adventure Club, scheduled to play that cancelled day of EZoo, told me. "I don't want to say it's a numbers games, but when there's that many people involved…I was watching a Louis CK show, and he said something like, 'There are so many people here, by the end of the month, one of you is definitely going to be dead.' It's a little morbid, but there is truth there."

It surprised me when Pasquale Rotella got nostalgic about the nineties. "There was something special about the simplicity of it all. I'm so grateful for how far Insomniac has come...but there was an intimacy to those early days, just like anything that starts out small and gets bigger." I asked him if he could remember his favorite parties from then. "Shiva's Erotic Banquet, Paw-Paw Ranch, Apocalypse...Paw-Paw Ranch even had a petting zoo."

A promotional documentary made by Insomniac Events called *Under The Electric Sky*, despite being a two-hour commercial for a festival (EDC Las Vegas) produced by the same company that puts on the event, got good enough reviews to get distribution in limited theaters. In it, we follow (in 3D) devoted fans to their destiny, EDCLV 2013. I watched the feature a few days before EDCNY. The participants include a misfit EDM fan from Texas and her boyfriend, a group of fratty guys, one of whom had recently overdosed and died, a couple who had met at EDC twenty years earlier and were getting married there, a loner who had lost the ability to walk and found therapy in dance music, and a polyamorous "rave family" of three men and three women who were also getting married, albeit not legally.

After the screening, my press group was invited to a pseudo-warehouse party complete with decorated freight elevator and go-go dancers. There were too many journalists there for it to be fun, but it was sort of educational. These promotional experiences are aiming, through fliers and old footage, to teach newcomers to this scene about rave roots and peaceful intentions. According to legend, there was a time when these pre-internet underground parties were about feeling—after one solved the scavenger hunt in order to find them—acceptance. Raves were like failed socialism, a dream too optimistic to come true in one try.

A note on all countercultures: each one follows a similar formula. 1. Create a scene by rejecting the predominant one and assign new music and graphics. 2. Assign a drug or euphoria, which could mean adrenaline, abstinence, religion, Special K, etc. 3. Make a secret language, which acts as a password. (If everyone is allowed in, there is nothing to get into.)

With other scenes, one had to perfect a context-dependent toughness. Finding the rave, though, was literally about knowing about a meet-up spot, a secret map that led to a secret party, which, once you were there, you were in. It was meant to be a wonderland free of judgment and grown-up rules, with all the fun parts of being adult still intact. So as long as you knew about the rave, you could be a raver.

As Rotella mentions in *Under The Electric Sky*, raves were for a very short time truly about a loving environment, and then they became a place for people to sell drugs. In creating the massive, multi-million dollar events like EDC that are commercially promoted, eighteen and up, and monitored by police, Rotella says he wants to create a similar mood to the one he remembers before drugs took over. The new parties are "definitely not superior. Each era of dance music had its own defining characteristics. Undergrounds were where it was at in the early days. That's all we had."

Despite everyone's insistence that huge electronic festivals have only the most positive of intentions, the lyrics to newer EDM songs are some of the darkest sentiments I've ever heard. Take Tiësto's 2014 hit, "Wasted," that goes, "I could stand you one more night; you are a catch twenty-two, either way I miss out, all of the grief I give you is energy I can live without; I like us better when we're wasted; it makes it easier to fake it."

Another example: in the Chainsmokers' 2016 track, "Closer," a man's voice sings, "I was doing just fine before I met you; I drink too much and that's an issue, but I'm okay. Hey, you tell your friends it was nice to meet them, but I hope I never see them again. I know it breaks your heart, moved to the city in a broke down car, and four years, no calls, now you're looking pretty in a hotel bar, and I can't stop. So baby, pull me closer in the backseat of your Rover that I know you can't afford, bite that tattoo on your shoulder, pull the sheets right off the corner of the mattress that you stole from your roommate back in Boulder, we ain't ever getting older." Next, a woman's voice responds with an only slightly more romantic refrain, sounding, in context, depressingly delusional, while hardly enthusiastic.

The melodies and imagery associated with these songs and countless others are, on the other hand, wildly hopeful. The contrast is jarring, especially as a huge, writhing crowd that is clearly dressed to hook up chants lyrics as pathetic-sounding as the German DJ Zedd's 2013 hit, "Stay The Night." It's as energetic as songs get, and the audience, when it comes on, goes crazy by fist pumping and jumping as sexily as possible against other sweaty bodies. But the words coming from their mouths are, "You kill the lights, I'll draw the blinds, don't dull the sparkle in your eyes, I know that we were made to break, so what? I don't mind. Are you gonna stay the night? Doesn't mean we're bound for life. So, are you gonna stay the night?"

EDCNY 2013 was massive, but not as big as the one shown in *Under the Electric Sky*, and so it felt like yet another preview. The music came from four different stages, one of which took me a whole day to find. A crowd of weathered and fresh-faced ravers eerily similar to the ones at EZoo stood under pouring rain the first day and blistering sun the second to jump and dance in front of the speakers that surrounded one or two far-off DJs. At the main stage an animatronic blue owl, the mascot of EDC, hovered over a booth. In order to fully experience the scene, I agreed to sit on the shoulders of a giant New Jerseyan covered in tribal tattoos. The owl's eyebrows rose. As the beat sped up and a countdown commenced, the owl's eyes crossed, then turned red, as if this was all too much. When the music reached the drop, the owl looked relieved, to my delight. During the next song, though, I was less convinced the owl's movements were synched to the music at all. Maybe it was the drugs.

Amidst amusement park rides and beer booths, candy-covered attendees crouched and lay down on the pavement in groups, their faces blank. Some wandered to the Chill Zone to find free water. In one tight crowd at a main stage set, I overheard a young woman say she felt dehydrated. "I literally have no water in my body. I need something to drink," she repeated, leaning on a shirtless guy. "I'll give you something to drink," he responded, high-fiving his shirtless buddy. Tiredly, she laughed too. In line for a ride, I saw two strangers exchange candy bracelets, joining curled fingers and outstretched thumbs to form a heart shape. Their expressions were as blank as everyone else's. Even the hardest dancers looked strangely serious, like they were working out.

A note on rave fashion: The gear is impractical, unflattering, and expensive, but it has a purpose. One exchanges homemade beaded "candy" bracelets to officiate a new friendship. Wristbands hide drugs. Gloves light up and look wild when tripping. One can rely on a pacifier charm to help with teeth grinding.

Sometimes I didn't get it, but at other times it would hit me: As Rotella said, everyone does their part in this community, this cross-section of New Jersey called EDC New York, representative, I agreed, of something much larger. Surrounded by shuffling, nodding zombies, I was struck by how strange it is we have to try this hard to escape our own routines in the first place, and how it is even stranger that the escape becomes another type of routine.

I never experienced the original momentum of raves, but I imagine they were, at their inception, a dream that breaking from a workweek could also mean breaking from reality: from consumerism, and essentially, time and space. Just because that dream was dashed doesn't mean that the rave can't live on, right? But in the twenty-teens, ravers raised to be business-minded in the face of a recession seemed even more hedonistic than their predecessors, when given the opportunity. Now, one is asked to spend hundreds of dollars on tickets and hundreds more on travel, refreshments, and costume, and to rely on this weekend of debauchery to fit nicely in a fenced-in area on one's three-day weekend. Childlike wonderment is something many would apparently do almost anything to recover, since as adults, we are told to control our own destinies. Festivals like EDC and EZoo (and Ultra, TomorrowWorld, and others) let us off the hook from that particular pressure. The transit is taken care of, the music is a numbing agent, and everyone can easily start fresh on Monday, scrolling past the hashtagged images as if they never happened.

Zedd was scheduled to play with Adventure Club and dozens more on September first, the last night of EZoo 2013. Just three days before New York's tragic losses, the second Zedd show of a two-night stop in Boston was cancelled after a nineteen-year-old girl died, and two more people reportedly overdosed at the House of Blues. On August twenty-eighth, Zedd tweeted, "Love and respect for those in pain right now. Our hearts go out to you." And, "PLEASE, everyone... BE RESPONSIBLE!" On September first, he tweeted, "I don't even know what to say anymore..."

Most DJs who play to thousands of people nightly don't do drugs. The human body can only take so much, and the more shows they play, the less opportunities they have to inhibit their senses. These guys party every night in different major cities all over the world, which means most of their time is spent flying. Often, they are booked for several shows in one day. For the most part, the other DJs I spoke to—Martin Solveig (whose hit goes, "I could stick around and get along with you, hello; it doesn't really mean that I'm into you, hello"), Sander Van Doorn (of "Love Is Darkness" and "Drink to Get Drunk" fame) DJ Sliink, and Flux Pavilion—seemed exhausted, more excited to talk about friends and family than drugs and parties.

Madeon, who got into dance music when he was eleven and started touring professionally when he was sixteen, said, "I genuinely don't see any drug usage. I'm an artist, and I'm only usually amongst other artists, and I don't really see what it's like in the crowd. I sometimes hear stories about people going to the hospital and I think that's a little bit of a shame. I think there are ways to enjoy these shows naturally. The thing is, I got into dance music when I was too young to party and to go out. As such, I always saw it as a musical culture, and I never associated the rave origins, really. I was kind of naïve."

At EZoo, a cylindrical LED show hovered over a smaller booth while a layered system of cutout screens surrounded another stage, all of them enhanced by 3D glasses being handed out at the entrance. Food booths served local upscale-casual choices like Roberta's Pizza and Bear Burger, and alcohol tents served Coors Light for nine dollars or a bottle of champagne for two hundred. Scrolling across a massive ticker over the English DJs Above & Beyond on the Main Stage West at the end of Day One were the words, "Whatever you do this weekend, remember to say yes more times than no."

In a clearly imbalanced ratio of men to women, male attendees with whom I spoke were coming from Pennsylvania, New Hampshire, Connecticut, upstate New York, and New Jersey, many of them recent graduates, amped on coming to the city to party with their frat brothers. Despite airport-style security checks, many were selling, asking for, and/or tripping on MDMA. A popular T-shirt slogan read "Have You Seen Molly?" and many other shirt messages were sexually explicit. I was invited to an EZoo after party in Times Square, which I was told was sold out before even EZoo was. Since it was on the cancelled day, I had enough energy to attend. Once at the massive club, I saw basically the same crowd from Randall's Island, only smaller and more fucked up.

If you know me, you know that these events are not necessarily my scene, but that I'm likely to say yes more often than I say no. At the end of each party, I found myself lost in the hedonistic energy of a crowd that—ill-intentioned or not—simply wanted to get away for the last days of summer, in a sky of confetti slowly falling through beams of white light. For the fourth or fifth time, I heard one of Zedd's hits, even if he wasn't there: "If our love is tragedy, why are you my remedy?" and finally felt the meaning: How can something this positive in essence end up so heartbreaking? A sea of hands reached up, and found no tangible answer, only another anticipated drop.

Right Place

In reality television, a narrative is always being reconfigured. An episode's beginning, middle, and end is not the same as the beginning, middle, and end of the recap that introduces the next episode. Different plot points appear when pertinent, and others fall away. The same conveniences apply to a TV star's image as a whole: a team of professionals control the parts of her that make the most sense to expose at the right times, and work to distract from or cover the parts that won't fit nicely into the agreed-upon story.

Imagine the first television shows were reality shows (docudramas). Imagine the format that became known as traditional for television and film was based on memoir instead of epic. Imagine a TV family born from the OJ Simpson trial and everything that made it so sensational: sports stardom, a mixed marriage, wealth disparity, race riots, live televised drama, and tell-all twists. Imagine a TV show born from a leaked sex tape, a TV star becoming an internet star, and vice versa. Imagine the TV is the internet and shows are three seconds long.

Kim Kardashian West's role in her show *Keeping Up With the Kardashians* is that of protagonist, and yet she is unsympathetic. She is required to drive plot forward, and yet her trademark is apathy. She is a character, but she is also a subject, or maybe more accurately, a theme. Something to be studied, through a long, thorough documentary about her life—a life that is always changing, based on the popularity of the show and its subject. Much of *KUWTK*'s chronology has been disproven by tabloids or blogs, like one called "Keeping Up With the Kontinuity Errors." But people, in general, cling to easily digestible linearity, and so the exposed artifice of the show hasn't stopped it from maintaining a coveted spot on old-fashioned basic cable.

Kim remembers a time before the internet, when cell phones were only made for people like her. Meet Kim, the reality television star who is happily playing the part of improbable icon, the ghost of Hollywood glamour reconstituted as the future of humanity. Kim has, more aptly than any piece of performance art perhaps—and surely for a longer timespan—reinterpreted the performativity of gender, race, class, and even the sex act. Her goal, it seems, is omnipresence. Kim is a collage of our old and emergent understandings of celebrity culture.

The most common consumption of the Kardashian drama is dispersed across platforms and timelines, and not via the sitcom-structured show, which is really the last voice to be heard, chronologically, in a continuous conversation with the family. The fallacy of that TV voice is apparent after less edited sources reveal information faster. But the show goes on, its structure still a comfort to many, likely including its own stars. Here, episodes are perfect arcs, consisting of a few conflicts and their resolutions.

Viewers who do their research know that the order in which these plot points occur isn't realistic, but for the sake of entertainment, we suspend our disbelief. The show's characters morph drastically from scene to scene, exhibiting different hairstyles, skin tones, and apparent bone structures by way of the latest trends in beauty routines. The shifts in facial features and body shapes manifest increasing cognitive dissonance that at once challenges a viewer's trust and mimics the hybrid lives of the show's stars. Nothing, for any of them, can be traced linearly, since everything they do is so much based on cacophonous, multivalent responses to their lives. Perhaps it is through the editing of their TV show that the Kardashians themselves can gain a sense of cause and effect, of time moving forward and not sideways.

In hundreds of think pieces about the Kardashians, writers have tried to pinpoint Kim's specific allure, struggling to understand how we, too, after hours of research, could end up gaining more of an addiction than an answer. It's the lack of affect that draws one in, like a black hole, many have concluded. It's a strange symmetry, or a beigeness, a voice described as the "sexy baby construct," a form of vocal fry. It's an emptiness that starts out scary and then becomes soothing white noise, like watching a car wreck float by to the perfect soundtrack.

It's true, Kim feels at once flat and multidimensional, her preferred self-image a flash photo taken at night. Her physical body is an improbable compromise. She's too curvy to be a model, and yet she's the most influential beauty ideal, only getting curvier. She appears, after all this unexpected success, to be keeping a secret that is larger than we can imagine. Kim is the giant salad she is always eating, the closed-mouth smile she flashes at jostling paparazzi, the impossibly flat midsection that hovers between impossibly round hips—a palette on which we place our insecurities about wanting too much. She's antifeminism incarnate and at the same time she is the most complicated of female portrayals, complete with unfathomable fears concerning overexposure and obscurity. She is extremely, uncomfortably selfish, and she published a surprisingly artful book called *Selfish*.

She's the epitome of narcissistic tendencies and seems to have no qualms about becoming emblematic of American greed. She's been described as a stereotype of shamelessness in an era intent on eliminating shame. Maybe she's not a void at all, but a surplus of the behaviors we were once told to suppress, like mixing business with pleasure by creating a personal brand that is inseparable from an interior life. But these facts alone don't explain Kim's own super-powers as a media figurehead, because celebrities who predate Kim did everything the same way she's done things, from the sex tape to the slogan merch. Paris Hilton's sexy baby voice and landmark reality television experiments are often credited as precursors to the Kardashian phenomenon, and yet, even if Paris is the same age as Kim, the latter's publicity empire plainly trumps the former.

Producers and the stars of the show (who have mostly become executive producers themselves) have insisted that the Kardashians are a real family with real problems, to be worked out honestly for the benefit of viewers. But it can't be ignored that they are an absurdly famous and absurdly wealthy family, with famous and wealthy family problems, to be worked out behind the scenes through business meetings. These meetings are then reenacted metaphorically for the cameras, through codified conversations that pertain more readily to a less famous and less wealthy audience.

Maybe we—the producers of the show and its critics—are both right. The Kardashians' successes do not feel attainable, but their lives, as shown on TV, are mapping out a highly contemporary family drama that has never been so clearly and consistently told. Following an older formula, we're being taught a newer narrative, one that suggests the future of media, business, and relationships. Therefore, the show must relate to everyone.

When asked what made her so famous, the narrative Kim likes to provide is the one about how the Kardashians have dealt with quite a lot, but they always keep it together. That the stem of the family's success is their unique closeness is of course ridiculous. The simple fact that some family members have left the show indefinitely, refusing to be part of it in the first place, or never having been asked to, should prove the opposite point. And yet writers tend to take the Kardashians and Jenners at their words. They're so friendly, we keep reading, while we watch reports of sexual exploitation, ultimate pretty girl cliques, and mafia-like ousting.

In an episode of the spin-off show *Life of Kylie*, Kylie Jenner says that if she and Kendall Jenner were not sisters, they would not be friends. The viewer's next thought is likely about whether any of the Jenners or Kardashians would be friends with one another if they were not related and famous for being so. One might wonder, next, if any of the peripheral characters—the best friends, the boyfriends, the girlfriends, the publicists, the assistants, the makeup artists— would be close to a Jenner or a Kardashian if it weren't for her fame. The answers to these concerns are inconsequential. The qualities in question are inextricable from the bodies that contain them.

As television viewing patterns change, so do the Kardashians. As media consumption patterns change, so do the Kardashians. They are nothing if not adaptable, and so, increasingly, the show focuses on what the show itself has done for the Kardashian brand, along with what the brand has done for the world, and how the lives of the family have had to change with fame. They've tackled stalkers, robbers, rehab, fan stampedes, bad press, exposés, knock-off merchandise, secret sex reassignment surgery, and fake friends.

Much of the content and merchandise created by the Kardashians is strategically unoriginal and even awkwardly over-branded. So many of their projects have tanked that their ratio of hits to misses is probably more interesting than their specific endeavors. The Kardashians take huge risks, small risks, and risks of every size in between. That their success rate in monetizing content is so high is due in large part to the sheer amount of projects they pursue. And they can pursue so many projects because they are in high demand, getting paid for promotional posts, public appearances, and exclusive photo series. The demand is not so much for a Kardashian woman's thoughts but for her crafted image, the behind-the-scenes quality that is part of the overall scheme. She shows her viewers the process of constructing and then selling her self, step-by-step. Consequently, we see that our appetite for a narrative of transformation informs the demand for a surface.

Where on the matrix of Art, Artist, Art Critic, and Muse, does Kim fall? With her Mona Lisa smile and sculpted form, she carries herself as a work in progress, crediting makeup artists and stylists, photographers, hairdressers, assistants, fashion designers, doctors, and her husband with constructing her. She is performance and pastiche, she is appropriation and readymade, she is a Factory Superstar. She's not exactly the "Marilyn Monroe of our time," as Kanye suggested, but maybe she's more like Marie Antoinette: unexpected, obliviously reckless, and destined for demise. She's like neither, really, but she's also like both. She's an easy emblem of an era. The era being, of course, late capitalism.

One way in which writers try to explain Kim's success is by placing her within a constellation of politics, art, and branding at large. Daphne Muller wrote in 2015 that "what is remarkable about Kim Kardashian is that the television show documenting her life, the Instagram and Twitter accounts that record her every move, and the virtual reality app game that allows users to engage in a fictionalized version of her life might as well be one and the same— every aspect of her life is a reflection, a performance, an abstraction of authentic lived experience."

Jerry Saltz wrote in 2013 that Kim could be included in what he calls the New Uncanny. She, Kanye, Lady Gaga, Jeff Koons, and Marina Abramović, he said, "are not just famous performers; they are performers of fame. In their grandiose sincerity, their attempt to keep it real ... these stars become alien things, automata, odd gods before our eyes. By some bizarre alchemy, they then toggle back into demented sincerity while simultaneously remaining alien, other, apart. They become psychological quantum particles, in two states at once. Sincerity and fame combine, float free of common rules."

It could be said that the Kardashians embody the fear of women: a fear of aging, of irrelevance, of being subsumed, or worse, of being de-feminized. Her body and its representations (perfume bottles, social media stickers, etc.) have become as exaggerated as ancient fertility totems. A repeated plot line on the show is the one in which a Kardashian sister is told by doctors that she cannot get pregnant and she is devastated. The takeaway is that she has struggled for what she has and is now discovering that she was struggling for the wrong thing.

It's the familiar narrative of rejecting independence for domestic bliss. Her success must not make her infertile. Her success must not overshadow that of her famous husband. In this narrative, Kim is a groupie at Kanye's concerts, a video vixen on the back of his motorcycle, a muse for his fashion line. She confesses that she is afraid to be too old to be all these things one day. At their engagement event, Kanye had a symphony play her favorite song, a song by another artist who aptly sells us back our own hunger for precarious femininity. The words aren't sung, but you can hear Lana Del Rey's ultra-vulnerable voice in the strings: "Will you still love me when I'm no longer young and beautiful?"

Another reality star, President Donald Trump, can be viewed as the other side of this coin. The oldest president in US history, Trump's constructed image is that of the recklessly masculine businessman who owns *Miss Universe* and is on his third wife—a wife who exhibits fear, only fear, behind her stretched eyelids. The fear inspired by Trump-like men is the same kind of fear that Lana sings about or that Kim ugly-cries about. In our darkest fantasies, we want to be good enough for a bad man, young enough for an old man, weak enough for a strong man, the sex object on the back of a motorcycle driven by a maniac.

Like the devil on one shoulder, Kim suggests, again and again, that we might be happier as all visual and no voice. Give in, she says, to the way the world is. As women, we are so controlled by the impulsive beauty standards set by consumerism, the only way to take back control is to become the standard by which beauty is measured. Consider for a moment that the Kardashians have always been close with *Girls Gone Wild* creator Joe Francis. Consider that Kim has said that she sided with her father, Dream Team lawyer Robert Kardashian, while the OJ Simpson trial was underway, while even her mother, Kris Jenner, sided with Nicole Brown Simpson's grieving family.

Women fear being happier in the role of accessory to a terrible man than in the role of businesswoman or superstar. Women fear being happy. And Kim is always walking that line, exhibiting both her drive and her regret. When asked if she'd rather be remembered as a sex symbol or a mogul, Kim responds, "Both. You can have it all." She will try to have it all, and we will watch and hope to see her fall. Because if she doesn't, that means we were wrong.

A lot of *KUWTK* takes place in doctors' offices. There, the women endure blood facials, in which one's own blood is extracted, spun, and injected back into her face. The image of a smiling woman covered in her own repurposed blood is too good of a metaphor for the height of self-centeredness. While some celebrities pose for photo-ops at blood banks, a Kardashian donates her blood to appear younger. It's unrelatable, say so many sources, and yet the treatment's popularity spikes.

bell hooks wrote in 2016 that "Beyoncé is the embodiment of a fantastical female power, which is just that—pure fantasy." But what of the fact that Beyoncé, writing lyrics about her husband, will always be more popular than her husband, writing lyrics about her? Or that Kim, using the medium of fame, can get more attention than her husband, who has mastered attention-getting stunts through music and fashion?

Male power is different than female power, these examples suggest. And if the media is seen as more powerful than government or even money, female power like Kim's is in fact stronger. Kanye has said that he wants to run for president. Kim, on the other hand, would never run for office. Switching gears from media mogul to politician would mean relinquishing some of the power she now has over the public. In 2015, she said to *Rolling Stone*, "I don't like to push my view. If I feel something, it's how I feel. I never say, 'I feel this way, so you should feel that way.' But, yeah. I think you would call me a feminist."

On *Life of Kylie*, Kris tells Kylie that she is the perfect role model for her generation because she has such a big heart. The audience knows that only half of this statement is true. Kylie is just as egocentric and materialistic as Kim, and she has the advantage of youth. But in some ways, Kylie, who has undergone body modifications to more closely resemble Kim, has become an antithesis, a funhouse mirror image of her predecessor. While Kim asserts that she was born to be in the spotlight, Kylie reminds us that she was born into it. Even when she was still a teenager, she was expected to make something of the massive following she accrued by stepping shyly into her family's glow. She cannot contest that any of this original attention was her doing, but she can feign reluctance to embracing it.

Kylie and the team at E! have come up with a persona that externalizes that personal dilemma of not being able to step away from fame. Kylie is playing up the younger millennial's fear of lost privacy, and to do so she must paradoxically be in public. She has accepted her part as anxiety-ridden outsider. Her plastic surgeries and her antisocial elite behaviors are mumbled contradictions, met with screaming rage in her comment sections. She's a symptom of Kim's virus, a reaction meme that has the capacity to become more relevant than the original.

"The man of the future will be of mixed race," Richard von Coudenhove-Kalergi wrote in 1925. "Today's races and classes will gradually disappear owing to the vanishing of space, time, and prejudice." This "race of the future" has since been depicted by way of composite photography, portraits of uncommon race combinations, and named actresses with a latte-complexion. The idea of a composite person is often presented as one with an oval-shaped face, dewy, golden skin, and bright, hazel eyes. Her high cheekbones are highlighted and her brownish pink lips puffy. Some versions have straight black hair and others have wavy hair in an ashy blonde. Some have a spatter of freckles, some have almond-shaped eyes. Some of these fictional women are simply described as looking like they are from Brazil (ironically, the country known as a plastic surgery capital).

This hypothetical woman is an idea of homogeneity, of perfection using politically correct guidelines. It takes into account that our current standards will dictate the survival of certain traits, and so all of these faces are conventionally attractive. Some of these faces look eerily similar to some of the faces of Kim. Because of the vast range of faces she's exhibited by way of makeover, Kim is every race and no race, smoothed and filled and bronzed and contoured beyond natural indicators.

Was racial transcendence her idea, or was it a makeup artist's? Did it come from her husband's Yeezy line's mixed race mood boards? How aware are any of the (part-Armenian) Kardashians, the (white) Jenners, the (part-Palestinian) Hadids, or the (part-black) Richies of this future race image they are projecting? The biggest models are lately olive-skinned, too. Their hair is slicked back, in braids, and/or not their own. Their eyes are brightened by contacts and their matte mouths are made poutier with collagen and bee venom. When a nose is not the so-called nose for one's race, is it the nose of another race, or of no race?

Like Madonna, who once held the title of queen chameleon, Kim was ridiculed for changing her style at first. But like everything else coming from the dramatic family and its societal ripple effect, the shifts became expected, normalized. Madonna owned the chameleon thing, but didn't market the evolution of her look as a mass product. The Kardashian brand, on the other hand, has become its own malleability. Glistening like a newborn and mummified in monochrome, the look is transitional, testing boundaries. Societal standards of beauty are indeed being challenged, but perhaps more importantly, we are seeing a shift in the way beauty is defined as a measurement. Beauty by definition has always had connotations of natural splendor. Faking beauty meant keeping the falsification a secret. If the secret was let out, one's intentions showed. Desperation to look beautiful was not beautiful, and therefore the filmed procedure failed at its task.

But Kardashians and Jenners are candid about some of their procedures. On the show, they get laser treatments, lip injections, Botox, and neck lifts in order to appear prettier for the very same audience watching them get work done. Treatments are more closely documented than the results. There is a contradiction of terms here. Appearing ugly—greedy, vain, and physically torn up or at least in pain—on camera will ostensibly cancel out so much of the gains that cosmetic procedures offer. To add insult to injury, these scenes are sometimes captioned with the huge sums that they cost. But since the women know and can afford the best doctors, the work must make them look beautiful. The logic stops there.

A similar contradiction: The Kardashians don't do their own makeup, and are wildly successful makeup moguls. Plenty of reality stars start businesses about which they know nothing, admitting to only lending their now-famous name to a product—all while being filmed for their reality show. The audience can see this process, and that the stars are cashing in on a fame that has nothing to do with designing handbags or aging wine, that they're simply getting fed ideas for deals and signing contracts. But the strategy usually works. The idea is that as an audience, we can no longer differentiate between advertising and authenticity because we've been made aware that businesswomen are forced to dissolve the line that separates the two.

The excuse for cosmetic procedures is always the same: it will help with her confidence. A woman faces the camera and says, "If you have the opportunity and the means to change something you don't like, why would you deprive yourself of that change?" But confidence is a code word here. In this screen world, eternal youth is expected and beauty is determined in numbers derived from a two-dimensional representation of the self. Kim even took the drag queen technique of contouring and made it palatable for her network TV audience. Her stretched face and her growing ass are simply ads for her product lines. She has made desperation a commodity to sell back to us, and therefore reversed some of the stigma.

So much of what the Kardashians do requires a savvy mind to play along with, if you're really taking in everything as marketing strategy. And you could, since almost everything we see them do is for money. Their brand is "working on my brand." The look is drag. They contour their bodies, too. On television, Kim was the poster girl for a sponsored lifestyle. Something about entrepreneurism, wrapped in a boutique she and her sisters ran that became a chain and then a few different spin-off shows. Something about getting this quality from their father, a lawyer and businessman, their mother/manager and her infomercials with their stepfather. But the truth is less passed down, more a response to the times. The attention from Kim's leaked sex tape had to be spun into something, Kris has explained. It was energy in search of an outcome.

In photo shoots, Kim has posed as Pamela Anderson, Cher, Cleopatra, Marilyn Monroe, Jackie Kennedy, Audrey Hepburn, Lil Kim, Marie Antoinette, and Jean-Paul Goude's version of the Hottentot Venus originally created for Grace Jones. Her very image is, she would like to have you believe, crowd sourced. She is constantly asking her fans what they think of her, as if she really was just a makeup tutorial vlogger this whole time. That's what she is right now because that's what's the most popular thing on YouTube. Later, she'll be something else.

As a character, Kim stands in for the fear we've always felt about the rich being happy and the limelight standing in for love. As a show and as a concept, *KUWTK* is comforting to the lower classes because it abstracts wealth by linking it only to empty fame. Perhaps the specific problems that the Kardashians face are too tragic to handle for someone less attention-hungry, we think. Living vicariously through them, we can tell that we're better off without the burden of all that. Kim will no doubt die one day in the name of vanity. But she will never die, of course. Her legacy will be an entire life, not just one iconic image or movie role.

Right Time

While working at a branding consultancy with fashion clients interested in YouTube stars and promoting the German translation of a novel I wrote that made predictions about new methods of fame and cultural leveraging, I heard countless takes on "influencer culture." I watched the first episode of a new Vice show hosted by obsolete prototype Paris Hilton, which tracks a social media star's path of fakery in search of making it, likening becoming a top tier personal brand to getting a dream role in Hollywood. I saw mass-market celebrities trail niche personalities when starting beauty lines. I read about the proliferation of branded selfie ops, "relative diminishing marginal aesthetic value," the first animated bot news anchor, and the limitlessness of media manipulation in the near future. All of this, while participating in and performing for multiple media formats myself, often with the goal of self-promotion.

I've noticed that a lot of people are somehow still under the impression that the influencer strategy of advertising doesn't affect them. Or they were under that impression until their daughter or friend or mother started the process of social media post-monetization. It's sort of like when you find out someone you know is selling products as part of a pyramid scheme, but this scheme is at least as all-encompassing as television and radio and print advertising combined. It's debatable whether influencer marketing is sustainable as a model. But for now, it seems that agencies will attach value to

(175)

every level of influence, and attempt to make gains from any or all of it.

In 2018, influencer marketing was old hat, a strategy that should have given way to something new by now. But, like cringey hashtag campaigns, it became ever more integrated into the advertising infrastructure it was supposed to subvert, or at least circumvent. Perhaps this boom, due to ad executives hoping to attract post-millennials, was driven by the teenagers they polled. For many, it was influence or die.

In the early summer of 2018, I received an email from a publicist about Vancouver's "influencer marketing and content platform" #paid (hashtagpaid.com), and although I hardly ever get baited by press releases, something compelled me to respond to this one. I was curious about the agency's processes, I said. The publicist suggested a phone interview with Adam Rivietz, the twenty-five-year-old co-founder and CSO. When I called, Rivietz was joined by his VP of marketing and PR, Richard Wong. Like any amateur journalist, my first question was how the startup started.

"A friend of ours, Ronnie, from Toronto, amassed over a hundred thousand followers in a year," began Rivietz. The year and platform in question are 2012 and Instagram, and the plural possessive referred to his co-founder/CEO, Bryan Gold, who was not on the call. Rivietz drew out certain words in a distinctive style I think of as pitch-speak, the impossible promise of relevancy. A clever tactic meant to simplify complicated explanations, each phrase is reduced to an emphasis: "We started analyzing what she was *post*ing, how her followers were re*act*ing. Commenters were asking her what *gym* she goes too, what *sports* bra she wears, what *pro*tein she puts in her shakes. She'd give them honest *ans*wers. That's when we stepped in and said, Hey, she's en*dor*sing brands without getting *paid*."

Influencer marketing is a multi-pronged term that includes mega-, macro-, and micro-, and each category comes with its own package of associative benefits. Influence is applied to everyone who has any type of following, from an average social media user to the most-followed person on a given platform. Everyone is susceptible to advertising, but if we all exhibit differing levels of influence, we also all exhibit differing levels of influence-immunity. Relative "authenticity" is a measurable factor here as well, the definition morphing into something like "engagement potential." The old advertising questions about efficacy and tactics remain, but when they're applied to the influencers, it's in everyone's interests to be portrayed as extremely normal.

Which is most effective: an influencer whose stock is high but whose motives are completely transparent, or someone subtler, whose earnest personal branding isn't easily distinguishable from sponsored content? Every social media user falls somewhere between the two poles. If anyone can be a potential source of "authentic" advertising, is anyone truly authentic online? These are not the kinds of questions that bothered Rivietz, who became Ronnie Friedman's manager when they were both nineteen. When I looked at it, Friedman's account @inspiredtobefit was a trove of before-and-after pictures that utilized all the old selfie tricks like better lighting, flattering bikinis, and self-aware posture. The food photos she posted were a mix of calorific desserts and colorful fruit salads. She often updated her followers on the health of her long-term relationship (now engagement!). In these photos, two grinning, blonde, blue-eyed high school sweethearts were always careful to make eye contact with the camera. To promote her e-commerce shop, she posted still life shots of the merch: pillows, mugs, totes, and framed posters with inspirational messages like "less greed more giving."

Not that I'm judging. We are all of us obligatorily familiar with and somewhat accepting of a double self-image: the contrast between a life and the image of that life as projected online. We each create a personal brand. We each author a narrative consisting of depicted moments. We sometimes wonder about the dichotomy between the moments we share and those we don't, how it relates to a truth, or a core, if those exist. What was authenticity, in another era? And what amount of authenticity is lost when we're promoting a cause, associating with a brand, selling a product—or selling ourselves?

When they first started working together, Rivietz, Gold, and Friedman compiled a list of ten brands Friedman either already used or wanted to work with. Rivietz reached out and brokered deals on his new client's behalf, at which point she was legally obligated to specify when her posts were sponsored with the words "ad" or "sponsored." But, says Rivietz, "it wasn't a stretch because we weren't forcing the brands at her. Her followers weren't surprised because she was already giving them product recommendations, since they were asking for it. Now, she's just earning revenue from these recommendations, versus the free replies she would write in her comments section."

Influence should be easier to determine than ever: follower counts tell the story, and analytics do the rest. But every good marketer knows that's not enough. If you're scrolling past an ad and land on a meme that's making fun of the flaws in the very same ad, your like might not be worth that much. In a vicious cycle, ads incorporate sarcasm and meme mimicry. This is how you get fast food Twitter accounts anonymously authored by comedians. Corporations, as they say, are people. And people, it seems, are corporations.

The dream of influencer marketing is to make ads from potential posts created by the kind of person who knows how to make their friends and family jealous. The goal is to blend in completely, to deploy a truly personal aesthetic, created by users themselves. The ideal user exudes an air that's aspirational but attainable. Her life is smoothed out and sunny, not overcomplicated with too many messages. She and her friends are just normal people having fun because of the products they've purchased.

I had heard the term "micro-influencing" before speaking with Rivietz and Wong, but probably didn't investigate its meaning. A micro-influencer, they explained to me, refers to a social media account that has a traceably better impact on its followers because it has a smaller, more trusting following than the typical movie star or name brand account does. Companies target smaller and smaller advertising platforms in order to set in motion word-of-mouth endorsements that people are more likely to believe. According to this logic, micro-influencers (or anyone with a following under a hundred thousand) are normal people who happen to be passionate enough about shopping to want to advise others on the quality of the products for which they shop.

Companies, from what I understand, pay influencers to promote their products in a way that each entity has agreed feels natural to their own brands. Companies could also send gifts to influencers, expecting but not contractually obligating a promotion, whether it be a YouTube review or a tabloid photo. Since the recipients of these gifts are not legally beholden to alert their fans of a paid promotion, the gift tactic serves as a loophole in two directions. First, unpaid advertisement ostensibly appears more authentic. To an influencer, though, a gift can add value to a personal brand. Posting a thank you note to a brand promotes the brand, but also one's self, suggesting one is important enough to receive free products.

To hear it from the guys at #paid, brands are doubly served by micro-influencer partnerships: followers are more likely to look kindly on a brand that contributes to the livelihood of a beloved non-celebrity. And a brand that invests in a personality comes to reflect that personality: a real, authentic person. The authenticity, whatever that means, bubbles upward.

Ronnie Friedman was #paid's first partnership. Her story has to be explained in the order in which Rivietz tells it, because if it's told in another, it starts to sound suspicious: "She started her Instagram account because she had a fitness journey, and the only way she knew that she would stick to that goal is if people were watching her. By posting every time she went to the gym or made a healthy meal, that kept her to her goal, which eventually got her followers, which eventually developed a powerful relationship between them, which allowed her to then monetize that fame."

What Rivietz was describing wasn't any more advanced or enlightened than product placement. Listening to him, I felt as if I was being asked to believe that a bunch of stars would have naturally put a Beats By Dre Pill Speaker in their music videos without the kickback. The timeline is, if at all valid, at least forced.

After the call, I got an email from Torri Webster, a twenty-one-year-old #paid content creator (her preferred title). "It's very rare that I would work with a brand that I had never tried," she wrote. She then listed her recent partnerships: Guess, Starbucks, Scotiabank, Puma, Covergirl, Bud Light, AT&T, Microsoft, Kijiji, Almay, Garnier, and Swarovski. It was hard to imagine all of these brands organically appearing in one person's life at one time. Most of Webster's Instagram images were shot by her cinematographer boyfriend, or, as she described him to me, "my 'Instagram husband.'" Her life looked as if it was sealed inside a snow globe, perfectly centered and in frosty tones. She had thick blonde highlights and made up her heart-shaped face with varying shades of tan. She was almost always laughing. She struck me, as most micro-influencers do, as the type of girl who was once very popular in a high school similar to my own Midwestern one. She could be one of the contestants on *The Bachelor*, I thought. The placed products were not difficult to spot in her feed.

Micro-influencers don't look like Hollywood superstars or fashion models. While elite celebrities are mostly super-thin, influencers are by contrast athletic and rounded. They flaunt their extravagant vacations, loving relationships, and stable home lives, even as they remain grounded enough to foster a large group of adoring friends. This is the lifestyle, it seems obvious now, America has always truly wanted.

"Unfortunately, the term 'influencer' can sometimes come with a negative connotation," Webster wrote. "I prefer to use the term 'content creator' because I think it encompasses what I do nicely. Being a creator is wonderful because it has given me the opportunity to gain interdisciplinary skills."

This brings us to the issue of Webster's move to New York City from Toronto, and to her burgeoning acting career (she starred in Canada's sitcom *Life With Boys* and played PeaseBlossom the Fairy in Nickelodeon's *The Other Kingdom*). With about three hundred thousand Instagram followers, Webster had crossed the threshold into macro-influencer status. According to studies, the bigger she would get, the more her engagement would level off.

#paid's Wong said, on the conference call, that thus far they hadn't had to worry about the shift from micro- to macro- to mega-influencer. For many clients, he insisted, sponsored posts are a side hustle to fund or inform a hobby, not a route towards stardom. He mentioned a flight attendant who got traction as a DIY pastry chef. But Webster, the first influencer client #paid offered to me for interview, mentioned her TV roles right away.

"I never want to pigeonhole myself into strictly one creative category (for example being an influencer or an actor)," she wrote. "I believe I can do both as long as my brand remains consistent. Overall, my social platforms have really helped with exposure and networking opportunities, but it is truly the quality of content and who you are in *real life* that really makes for a long career."

Before it was a traceable statistic, "influential" used to mean "cutting edge." But an influencer isn't influential in that way anymore. A typical influencer today is basic—the opposite of avant-garde. She's the affluent, pretty person you'd rather not admit you pay attention to, because she is, by default, a sellout. Still, although you may not even know her name, there's something about her skin that makes you sick with envy. She's not plagued by celebrity scandal or even a career, and yet she's incredibly, impossibly popular. In the daydreams of her followers, she wakes up every morning to an excess of opportunities, each more fun than the previous one.

Does the micro- or macro-influencer sell happiness? She's not famous for her talents—at least not yet—but she's still being paid to document her lifestyle. Her influence is acute; it's measurably more powerful than the effect a big celebrity might have on her millions of fans. Because she is a no one, she's someone. It's this type of person—not her much wealthier or more famous colleagues—that is our era's real trendsetter.

"Influencer" is what we're calling them now, but that's just one in a timeline of those words invented to describe celebrities who are first and foremost talented at utilizing new media. The linguistic evolution has taken zeitgeisty terminology from alluding to the dramatic to pinpointing the vanilla. In other words, we've gone from coveting the few to the many, or the iconic to the algorithmically induced.

"Influencers" were once called "it girls"—a term I never thought I'd miss. After speaking with #paid, though, I reread Jay McInerney's 1994 *New Yorker* profile "Chloe's Scene" to try and remember what it used to mean to be influential and young. McInerney famously names Chloë Sevigny "the coolest girl in the world," based on her ability to spot and insert herself into trends: a Sonic Youth music video, Larry Clark's first movie, a Maison Martin Margiela fashion show, Bernadette Corporation's short film. In the profile, the high schooler is effortless, unreachable (she doesn't have a pager yet and is hardly ever at home), and in-demand.

In this day-in-the-life story, Sevigny chooses modeling for indie magazines over *Vogue Italia*, since, as McInerney describes it, "'Down low' is a cherished concept: secret, alternative, not commercial—everything one wants to be. Except one also sort of wants to be famous, and here is the contradiction at the heart of Chloe's world, the dilemma of subcultures that ostensibly define themselves in opposition to the prevailing commercial order, the dilemma of all the boys and girls who want to be in *Paper* and *Details*: What do you do if *Harper's Bazaar*, or Calvin Klein, comes calling? In Chloe's case, so far, you sort of blow them off." Twenty-four years later, she wouldn't. Who would?

The press release that prompted me to call Rivietz, Wong, and their publicist was about a Nielsen Report that promised to break down the benefits of influencer marketing and explain what the trends say about where it's heading. Clearly the formula was working: everyone was making money and getting free stuff. But was anyone they were describing cool?

"Being sponsored has always been cool," said Rivietz, the self-described tech-preneur. There's a stigma, he clarified, attached to paid posts on social media, but, like any type of advertising, it would become less jarring the more we saw it. He recalled his youth, when he and every other skateboarder he knew dreamt of being sponsored. In my experience (I'm seven years older than Rivietz), some young skaters certainly liked the idea of sponsorship, but plenty of others called it what it was: selling out.

As another example, Rivietz described the difference between the guys in his high school who were against making "catchy songs or anything commercial" and the bands he was in. "They're like, I don't wanna be a sellout, I don't care if my music ends up on the radio. We said, 'Well then you'll never make money in the music business.' They wanted to be the true artists; they want their creative freedom. There's always that battle, in any creative field. Some people are willing to sell out a little more."

In his pitch, Rivietz had spun the refusal to sell out as irrational and maybe inauthentic. "Another way to view this is," he continued, "[marketers] are giving money to help support that *crea*tor to create even more amazing content that their audience *loves*. So from the audience's standpoint, it's not like [creators] are paid for a *pro*duct placement, it's more like a *valida*tion. It's that this amazing brand believes in the creator—person—that I follow, and now they're helping that creator make a living. It's about the creator continuing to make content. That's the change, in terms of the mindset." As if in conclusion, he added, "I don't really think it's about selling out anymore."

The rationale was cyclical. Entertainers must earn money, and the entertained must pay up, in some way. "Even if you don't have a significant following, you understand that if you expect someone to create a weekly YouTube video or post on Instagram every *day* and commit their *lives* to creating content for you, then they need to make money *some*how."

As he compared paid posts to charitable acts, I could hear Rivietz almost start to believe himself. Many agencies, including #paid, promise a seamless monetization of social media posting: Get paid to do the hard work you're already doing, by providing the world with engaging content, their mission statements all say, in so many words. Your brand is already established, they coax. If you're not making money from it, you're working for free.

This fair-is-fair explanation is not really how economies work, including the attention economy. Still, countless startups will hinge their success on managing these projections. Meanwhile, talent and creative agencies have scrambled to rebrand as specializing in influencer marketing. On hashtagpaid.com, an interactive slider calculates how much you can make per post based on average engagements. A button below it encourages visitors to "start getting paid" by joining the fifteen-thousand-strong "creator marketplace" established across over one hundred countries.

For Webster, the promotional life is a form of preparation for whatever comes next. She doesn't see herself doing paid posts forever. "I am already seeing a shift in the social media world, and these platforms will surely give out on all of us eventually."

Rivietz started his career "in the twelfth grade" with a company that targeted the most popular kids in school ("the influencers of their grade" before that was a term) and had them sell prom packages to their classmates. Inspired by a Facebook friend who made his first million in high school by outsourcing app development to India and by a book called *Millionaire Fastlane,* he dropped out of college to create his first app suite. His company, called Entourage Apps, was named after his favorite television show. "I've always wanted to be [*Entourage* character] Ari Gold," he said, talking faster when he was asked about his own life. "And now, to some extent, I am." Meaning, he explained, that he never wanted to be famous, only to be able to affect billions of people from behind the scenes.

As someone who must think about this stuff all the time, I wondered if the dystopian idea that every part of one's life could be monetized kept Rivietz up at night. "I mean, it does. But if you're on the founding side of it, you can choose how you want to guide the industry, what governing bodies you're going to work with to maintain standards."

He was the one who brought up *Black Mirror*. "In season three, episode one, a woman is trying to maintain her score to live in a particular condo building—and there have been talks in the news about China rolling out a very similar program where everyone will be able to vote on everyone's social standing, and your rating will impact what loan you can apply for, what mortgages you can get, what jobs you can get, where you can live. That is scary, to me. But on the pro side, or the not-so-scary side, I don't think it's a problem that people are concerned about what other people think if it means they maintain a higher level of respect for others, or if it reduces the amount of profanity people use."

He paused, and then added, "There are definitely pros to having people watching over you, just like our friend Ronnie."

I was the one who brought up scandal-plagued YouTube stars PewDiePie and Logan Paul, both of whom had gotten called out for extreme racial insensitivity. Richard Wong responded, "In terms of letting the fame get to them—you have some people who go through those kinds of issues, and they just need to be coached.

They understand that this is a privilege, to work with some of these brands. We haven't really encountered any times when they've been way too big and want to leverage anything." #paid advised corporations to not place every egg in one unstable basket, he said. "When you're working with one big creator, if that creator goes off the rails or becomes less well-liked as a brand, that's a big issue. We encourage brands to work with a roster of creators, generally between thirty and fifty. You can have an accident or a personal crisis—a family emergency, or a natural disaster in the area where a creator is living. The best way to safeguard is by having a diverse roster, that you can easily sub one person in for another."

Another way to put this is that influencers are interchangeable. It shouldn't have surprised me, then, when, soon after I started speaking with these agency people, a bot named Lil Miquela was hailed as the world's first successful CGI influencer. Miquela followed in the footsteps of popular Japanese holographic animation Hatsune Miku, who amassed fans through live concerts instead of social media. Miku was a fashion darling for a short time, appearing in ad campaigns alongside the CGI hero of Final Fantasy games. But Miquela's strength was not her cutting-edge technology, but rather her interactive story.

In her frequent posts, Miquela forms a personality, interests, hobbies, and friends. She "moved" to New York from Los Angeles to pursue fashion collaborations, which were already being offered to her by Prada, Glossier, and others. At over one million followers, she became a mega-influencer.

Miquela was developed to be a maximally authentic non-person. Described as half Spanish and half Brazilian, she has the coffee complexion of those dated predictions of what everyone in the future will look like. She was nineteen, she told us, while complaining about the wispy hairs that fall on either side of her head beneath two Princess Leia-like buns. The existence of Miquela suggested that all influencers were phoney, which, as told by graphic, somehow read as honest.

Sometimes, Miquela would mention a brand, and other times she wouldn't, but a brand would be prominently featured in a post. She never specified a post as paid-for, probably because as a non-person, she didn't have to. Like an authentic influencer, Miquela was sometimes "depressed," and reached out to her followers for support. She would get it, in the form of hundreds of comments from actual people who insisted she was as real as anyone else they followed.

As the year 2018 trudged along, I thought about my conversation with #paid but didn't want to revisit it. I tried to watch a reality show about a gamer girl wanting to "cross over" to makeup collaborations, who held meet and greets in video game stores where fans lined up to hug her and cry. She was pretty, and an influencer in a field with one of the most notoriously horny comment sections. When a producer on the show asked her about raunchy messages she received, she brushed off the question with a short explanation about the cloak of anonymity and how it can embolden people. She couldn't let violent threats bother her and continue her work. Her brand was clean and innocent, even though she was under a thick layer of concealer and inundated with lascivious text.

Miquela "modeled" for magazines, did platform takeovers, and got signed by a record label. She got a "tattoo" by a real person and "attended" festivals like something called Beautycon LA. At a fashion week party, I spoke with a model represented by the same agency as Miquela. The people who created her, he said, are cool, and therefore she's cool, a good role model for teens that want to look up to someone "not sample sized." But she's not a size at all, I countered, or a person. She won't age, scar, burn, or get acne, and yet she promotes beauty products.

In fact, looking back on the first Lil Miquela posts (which have since been deleted), I noticed that she started out much less realistic, with an impossibly small waist. Later, she became more freckled and preferred baggy clothes (although her proportions—not to mention her "skin"—still seemed pretty unattainable). Miquela was taken seriously as an influencer because she was effective. Her fans were captivated. And how could they not be? She was well written and beautiful and had smart style. That she wasn't a person didn't really matter because at some point, every person becomes an avatar in the mind once our main interactions with them are via social media feeds. That she wasn't even a projected hologram like Hatsune Miku or an all-star music group's cartoon collaboration like the Gorillaz didn't matter, either, because concerts weren't as popular as they used to be. That she was selling products didn't seem to bother anyone because, as Rivietz predicted, the brands that supported her were in on something.

But the real benefit to creating a bot as the ultimate influencer was that she could change shape with evolving trends. Her mood considered the climate. She was angry at prejudice against her "race," for example, until she discovered that she was not human and became conflicted about deciding if she had one. In April, Miquela's Instagram account was "hacked" by another bot, a blonde Russian rightwing CGI influencer named Bermuda (@bermudais-bae's bio: "The earth isn't getting hotter but I am"). For days, Bermuda posted the "truth" about Miquela: that she wasn't real, not even based on a real person, like she thought she was, and created by "a literal genius moving this country forward without any real thank you or acknowledgement." She linked Cain Intelligence, the website for "the industry leader in Conscious Language Intelligence (CLI), a type of Artificial Intelligence that allows for humans to engage with our specialized robots in free-format, natural language."

In the interactive drama, Miquela eventually regained her account from Bermuda, and most of her old images reappeared there (that's when her oldest, most Sims-esque selfies went missing). A post thanking fans for their support during the "hardest week" in her life described the process of discovering that she was a "robot." "I was built by a man named Daniel Cain in order to be a servant. Brud stole me from his company in Silicon Valley and 're-programmed' me to be 'free.' But they're the ones who define my freedom through THEIR technology." The post got emotional, and in the comments section, thousands of followers told Miquela that she was still real to them, that she still inspired.

This was the start of a science fiction that could go in many directions. Was Russian troll Bermuda lying, and to what end? Was Daniel Cain an Eldon Tyrell-like villain and were some androids, like in *Blade Runner*, still blissfully ignorant of their inhuman forms? Are we, all of us, as phoney as the bots we're following? Almost every day, the characters were reconfigured to add a twist to the plot, with Miquela at the center as a hero, questioning her makers, her friends, her reality. Throughout the story, Miquela would wear visibly branded clothing and promote editorial cameos, paid partnerships, and living humans.

The joke was on us, the consumers, who believed in an ideal influencer. After complaining about unrealistic beauty standards for decades, examples like this have proved that we collectively stopped trying to police impossible aspirations in advertising. Authenticity is an affect. Anyone we know could be pseudo-secretly advertising to us. While micro-influencers pose behind a moneyed veneer, even our most unpopular friends repost ads in order to gain discounts on products. No matter how easy it is to see the façade, it is inseparable from the image. Even if the story of an influencer becomes a cautionary tale about the singularity, collaboration contracts were signed, and as an outcome, products were sold.

The scariest part of *Black Mirror* episodes is always that the victims of technology are destroyed by their complicity. We know it's not real, but when we buy it, we are making it real. As Miquela pleaded in her return to Instagram, "I'm not a human, but am I still a person?" The answer, in a list of responses below her question, was an awkwardly heartfelt "yes."

Engagement

Safeway

I'm alone at Safeway and overhear, "They're taking Four Loco off the shelves."

"I know," says a girl I know is named Helen.

"It's fucked up."

"We should get some before they're all gone."

"It's not that kind of night, bro."

I pick up a magazine, which is the equivalent to an eye roll in a supermarket, maybe. No one is looking at me. Do they know that I know her mother, who worked in my office?

"It's too early to get the turkey."

"We should get it anyway. Before it's too late."

Hypocritically, I drank Four Loco the night before last night, and I'm thinking about Thanksgiving, too. But my cart has only cleaning products and flavored mineral water and a fifth of Seagram's gin. I'm holding a Starbuck's large iced coffee: milk, no sweetener. I never get sweetener. I sometimes want it, but can't bring myself to say it. Holding a large Starbucks cup is somehow hypo-critical, too. Or it's something I'll do for the rest of my grocery shopping life, and that's it.

As much as I tell myself I don't care what people think of what I'm buying, I always end up with a cart half full of produce. I put the toilet paper on the lower shelf.

"We didn't get sweet potatoes."

"I don't know what to do with—"

"We can wrap them in plastic wrap, put them in the microwave—"

"Jim. Don't. Start."

I sometimes buy potatoes. It seems like everyone does. We walk past the sign that says ".69/lb." and we have to say why not. The potatoes—every kind, and squash, too—have to look okay. There is no way that I know of to check if one will taste good, but we all always take the phallic looking ones, or the perfectly round ones. I want mine straight and even. I don't want the tip to taper to a wisp.

I get home and start to make a stir-fry. I rinse mushrooms, thinking, mushrooms don't need to be rinsed, unless they have dirt on them. Something about the thin skin? I slice them and they quietly slip away from my fingers like little tops. I feel a swelling of emotion and wonder if it will slip away, too, and if I would have felt it if someone else were here. The potatoes stay in the basket on the counter. I'm invited to a party that will happen later. I'll bring the gin, and I'll drive myself there and back, picking up friends and dropping them off.

* * *

I go to jail after a DUI arrest. It is not a dramatic ordeal when I go in, but it's still scarier than I could have prepared for. I am walked down an awful hall full of echoing voices and smells that seem to echo. It was as if my whole driving life was spent worrying about coming to this place for this reason, and now it had happened. But now I would have to worry about a lot more. I'd have to tell everyone at work what a fuck up I was and hope to not get fired for missing a day. I'd have to catch up once I got back, and catching up would be harder because I'd have appointments to add to my schedule. I'd have to breathe into a device periodically while driving, even during the day, and I'd have to make sure to never do this again, beyond the point of the device being removed and my PO leaving me alone. Things would only be worse for me then.

One of the women is middle-aged and overweight. She looks like she's developed a dumbed-down kindness that she relies on. She looks like she never even considered getting thin or getting rid of the gray streaks in her hair. I'm surprised by how friendly and vacant she can look in a place like this. I know that because I've met her in jail and she doesn't appear it now, she is incapable of appearing thoughtful.

Another is the brassy bottle-blonde type I'd expect to see here, but she gets quiet in a way that's almost pathetic, too. She still frightens me. I don't learn any of their names. Usually, I'm good with names. I busy myself by pretending to read the scratches on the walls and trying to appear apathetic and uneducated.

"They look fine, I checked. What's on the menu tonight?"

"Sasha's inta trying new things all of a sudden."

"My kind of girl."

"I gotta let you read this book she just gave me."

I am momentarily happy, thinking about the cliché of two guards talking about what their wives were cooking. A woman with tight brown curls and a wide part going from the middle of her forehead to where she would start to bald if she were a man talks the most, and it's about her son, who is only ten but he's so funny, not just for a kid. She talks about missing him now and while she works—she's a hostess at Furr's Cafeteria—but that she doesn't mind her job, never has, it's better than this place, that's for sure.

"I didn't take my glasses in here with me. My sister was all, don't take those, and I didn't know why she'd say that, but now I get it. I don't even want to see it, you know?"

I mean, I'm here, too, sitting on the ground instead of the benches, which are taken. No need to consider the differences between the colors of collars. No need to talk about life outside. We only have this time together. Maybe I should tell a story about drugs or a guy that hurt me.

"I could use a drink."

"Right? Seven and Seven's mine. Thas my drink, right there."

"I like the smooth stuff. You're like my husband, you like the harder stuff."

We've been here for hours, talking in small bursts, always ending with Middle-part getting half-voiced sounds in response to her tapering anti-climaxes. She looks like she's repeating something to herself silently now. Overweight looks pained. Maybe she's thinking about the horrible possibility that in order to talk, she would have to complain. Brassy is frowning, and a girl who is probably under twenty-one is staring at her wrists, cross-legged in a corner. We are all in a corner, really. Outside, at, say, a family party or a church bake sale or a school field trip, we'd all feel this way but have the background noise of socializing to help us forget. Here, if it was too late to start talking, it meant you'd be silent for, in my case, eleven hours.

"My husband wants to go to Canada. I'm like, what's there? Sounds cold."

"I'm from Canada. I'm an Army brat," says the youngest girl.

"My dad says I'm an Army brat and just a brat. He said he'd never bail me out, even if he could. He can, though, and he can afford it."

"I can't wait to get out. My son is gonna be so worried. I can't even wait."

No need to try to figure out if others are starting to realize how insane it would probably make a person if they had to listen to the obvious said aloud every fifteen minutes forever.

* * *

I no longer have a job and to celebrate, I oblige my now ex-coworkers when they ask if I want to go to a strip club on my last day.

"Let's give it up for Candy, Candy, Candy. Isn't she sweet?"

Nothing sounds like conversation here. Nothing is said aloud except for thoughts on what it is we're doing and what it is they're doing. This is because none of us are being honest with each other: None of us are all the way comfortable here, and that our degrees of sympathy for the dancers vary is also an uncomfortable thing to consider.

"Tiffany is coming up next, and I know you've been waiting for that. Right now we have the lovely Jasmine, let's make her feel right at home."

One of us gets a lap dance in the back room. He is silently othered.

A girl pushes her tits in my face and shakes them. They feel velvety, not like baby's skin but softer. I think they shimmer. She looks ageless, and much prettier up close. If I had seen her walking at Safeway, I would think it was too much makeup, but it is perfect for this lighting. Her movements start at the rounded platforms strapped to her toes and glide upwards like a slow motion whip.

The next girl is flat-chested. She pulls at her bra as if she doesn't believe this. I want to see the irony, the cinematic decadence crawling over the layers upon layers of skuzz. I instead see the secret humiliation on either side of the stage, the smiles that don't get answered, the stories about school and always wanting this kind of attention and making friends you couldn't find anywhere else in the world and an understanding boyfriend who loves to come here, but only to see her. I want to see defiance, but I can only see the ignorance of the argument. How typical of me.

"Let's give it up for Tiffany, Tiffany, Tiffany."

She walks on stage and it's like watching a girl on the sidewalk at a time when no one is walking on the sidewalk. But Tiffany is switching between pouting and smiling, trying to convince me that her outfit looks fine in this false daytime, and that she doesn't even know why they call it a "walk of shame" if it's fun.

This context renders it inappropriate to talk about sex. I start to think about human evolution and I wonder what these thoughts are doing for my species' existence. Like the instinct to encapsulate. Or the urge to fall in love with one's own ideas. A now ex-coworker, Jeanne, and I are the only two women not performing here, and we're at the same table, a few feet away from Tiffany. We somehow start talking about the pharmaceutical industry. We sit like slumping piles next to this stretching ideal. We are assaulted by all levels of intimidation, and laughing, not sure when to look and for how long. I feel so much weight and darkness pushing past us: we are on Mars and the girls are on the moon.

Another coworker gets up to follow a girl to the back room to get a lap dance. I know that this will be something whispered about, and he must know this too, and something has ensnared him into imagining that this will be worth those whispers. Maybe he's just following suit. He is of lesser rank than the first coworker who went back there. Not that it has anything to do with me, because I'm gone.

"You ever been on the back of a motorcycle?"

"A couple times," I say, not knowing where this conversation is going.

"What about for six hundred miles?"

"No."

"I think you're going to like it."

The holidays are over and he doesn't have to go back to work yet. I sit behind him on his motorcycle and we pick up speed, through and out of my city and into the desert. The only noise: the engine, the only communication: movement, which is dangerous. I see my obscured face in his circular mirror and notice I'm smiling and pale.

Plots of movies we've seen and discussed run through my head as the prickled landscape burns past us. *True Romance*, *Wild at Heart*, *Written on the Wind*. People like us always watch movies like these, and then talk about how love can't possibly exist. What a fantastic thing it would be if it did. What were our parents thinking, having children? What is anyone thinking, moving in together? The desert was always so threatening and vast, but now it seems to roll on like encouragement.

At a diner called Great American Food in Why, Arizona, we suck on Coke from straws because it seems appropriate. He doesn't even like Coke, he said a few days ago. I ask what kind of movie this would be if it were one.

"A road movie, obviously, so, it would have to be coming-of-age."

I don't mention The French New Wave because it was too quirky, too close to believing in love. What would he think of me? I'm no daydreamer. "Are we going to come of age by the end of this?"

I know we've played out those kinds of plots in other experiences, because I met him when he was on his first road trip. He and our mutual friend Jake had dropped out of high school and ran away from home. For a week they stayed in my garage, where I had to hide them from my parents. We remember different parts to that story: I was impressed that he'd just left without telling anyone; he was impressed when I'd been trying to impress them by sneaking out at night to see an older guy who gave us all Ritalin. This is the first time we've seen each other since. He tells me that he was a virgin then. We decide it would have been perfect if he had lost it to me.

Back on the motorcycle my thoughts never become focused. They loop like the chorus of a song, sometimes interrupted by new scenery. Before we left, we bought helmets at the Honda store and they came with booklets that advertised colored visor inserts, fog-reducing plastics, and an earpiece that made it possible for riders within 500 feet of each other to have conversations. I suggested it, but later agreed that it wasn't really the point. If I had wanted that kind of a road trip, I could have left with my friends in a rental car. Instead, I waited for him to take motorcycle-driving lessons and to get the bike and the license. He told his mother about the trip when we went to her house and used the old desktop to Google-map the smaller highways.

"You're not going to bring music, or anything?" she asked.

She is this classic unemployed divorcée who somehow ended up with the house, the Mercedes Benz, and the two mastiffs.

"No, mom," he said gruffly. "I just want to zone out."

"Me too," I said. I like his mother, but I like filling the role of the girl who took her son away from her better. He already escaped her at seventeen, and somehow I had become involved then. Now, at twenty-eight, if he died on this trip, his mother would see it as a story of too much rebellion. And I'd be dead with him.

That we met again through unplanned circumstance must have been what convinced him to invite me on this trip at all. I know he has loose ends to tie up in other states and that these do not involve me, cannot involve me, are probably the factors that brought him closer to and further from me, but will not be spoken of on a trip like this one. I have some shit of my own I won't bring up.

The more we stop and have these brief conversations, though, the more we have to be conscious of ambiguity. This is the getting-to-know us stage, and so we are supposed to talk about how we are.

"Me, I'm the type to…" and "I usually never… but…" I try not to say anything that isn't somehow a question, and I focus on the present. We want this to be different.

"The better you know a person, the less you like them," he says.

"That's why relationships are actually unromantic," I say.

"I've been told I just set 'em up to knock 'em down," he says about girls.

"Most guys tell me they're in love with me *after* we've broken up," I say.

Of course this is a competition, this long flirtation.

Even where we stay is debatably ironic (a Best Western, which his mother would call tacky). I'm confused when he decides on Red Lobster for dinner. "It's pretty bad," I say, my mouth full of Lobster Nachos.

"Of course it is," he says, holding a twenty-two-ounce glass of Heineken. "It's about the experience." He keeps saying that.

Finally, we're met by the soft, soft white of two queen-sized beds (that we push together). I sit down and look out the window, so sore I almost can't move. Should I recount dusted mountains and corrugated side-roads, the uninhabited Dateland (our "first date"), the puckered roadhouse staffs and the intimidated young store clerks, the photos we took of each other when we ran out of gas in the Tohono O'odham reservation, or "T.O. res" ("When will this stop being exciting?" he said, with one thumb to the road, helmet cradled in his other arm), as we rest our aching legs and backs and arms in the dried up strip mall called Yuma, with the hotel and the Red Lobster? We instead have sex, welcoming the contrast of wide-open and pillowed.

On day two we become distant from every other thing, and so, close. I wonder if we both lived in the same city now if we would notice each other. We are ecstatic about the tiny road that goes up and around a hill that has spruces, a slick little gray wolf, and chunks of snow clogging edges that we tip towards.

* * *

I am in pain because I'm slipping off the back. I know I won't fall but the metal thing is digging and vibrating. It's getting dark and we're in the carpool lane hitting L.A. traffic. I can't tell him to look at the sunset happening on the ocean or the pink highlights happening on the mountain and more importantly I can't tell him to pull over because I am in pain. My helmet becomes a balloon, keeping in my tears and whimpers, collecting moisture and suffocating my independent thoughts. When we pull over for gas, he says, "Did you want to get off sooner?" about my tugging at his jacket. I nod and feel feminine in the most ugly way. He does not make it better at first, reprimanding me for being unsafe, but then he lets me pump the gas and suggests we take a very long break before getting back on the road, even if we're this close. We drive to the nearest mall because it has a movie theater and joke about the people we startle in the parking lot with our visors up, the first time we've talked while riding because we are going so slowly. At a stop sign he squeezes my thighs with both hands. I wonder if he can see in the mirror that my eyes are red.

* * *

We go to the Museum of Jurassic Technology. We are overwhelmed by the meanings and possibilities presented by every turn, and even wonder if the two out-of-order bathrooms are part of the exhibits. We ask the docent if we can leave our helmets somewhere and he puts them in a storage closet full of objects I can't take seriously because of the nature of this place. He then tells us that the Center for Environment and Land Use next door will have a bathroom. When we are outside we talk about how everything looks weird because of the way that place was making us think. We look closely at vine-covered walls and large glass doors, smoking cigarettes. Inside the building next door, a grid of sixteen TV screens displays panning views of boring landscapes.

Another wall is covered in brochures. A small table in the middle of the room has a carpeted top. A black cat sits there. I offer my downturned palm and she rears up like a tiny horse, smacking my hand with her head. A man appears behind a desk and directs me to an area that looks like a drafting studio. "It's the door with the ladder on it," he says. We shuffle out and see the docent from the first museum step in behind us, holding take-out Chinese.

My favorite exhibit is a video about Geoffrey Sonnabend— who conceived the idea for this series, "Obliscence: Theories of Forgetting and the Problem of Matter," immediately after attending what happened to be the final performance by the singer Madelena Delani, who drove off a cliff.

His favorite is an audio and still photo documentary of Madelena Delani's short life. Both are hysterically boring and sloppily rendered, and they make us think about coincidence and memory, which is hard, even with a model to look at called "the Cone of True Memory (by which the being experiences experience)" and its counterpart, "the (Class One) Plane of Experience," which is always moving from "the Obverse Experience Boundary" to "the Perverse Experience Boundary."

Just that I am talking to him about this and that he is interested and understanding makes me feel less like a girl who rides on the back of a motorcycle. We talk a little about the head trauma he suffered from a bicycle accident as a child. He has a faulty short-term memory, which he describes as "a beautiful excuse." It intensifies all memories before the accident, he says. I haven't noticed. In fact, he is better at remembering stuff from our shared past, and from yesterday, than I am. "Maybe it's all the drugs I did in high school," I say.

"Maybe you just really don't care," he says.

I have to bunch my dress up to get back behind him. It's dark and he splits lanes, which scares me.

I've stuffed everything I brought with me into my helmet. He offers to buy it from me, not saying why he'd want an extra. I say I want full price and he says no way, not for a used helmet. I say I'd rather use it as luggage than get ripped off. I get into a cab to go to the airport. "See you later," I say, accidentally.

Out of State

Spike Art magazine: In 1980, the French newspaper *Libération* asked Marguerite Duras to write a chronicle for them over one year. The pieces could be as long or short as she liked, so long as she wrote every day. Duras said a year was far too long and proposed three months instead. "Why three months?" her editor asked. "Three months is one summer long," she replied. "Agreed, three months, but every day," the editor insisted. Duras didn't have anything planned for the summer and almost gave in. But then she suddenly became terrified that she couldn't plan her days as she wished. So she said, "No, once a week, about whatever I want." The editor agreed. For the summers of 2017 and 2018, we invited Natasha Stagg to do the same: one text a week, of any length, on whatever she likes.

* * *

In Berghain, the corridors reminded me of an early RPG game, maybe because of the mushrooms I was on. Characters in leather harnesses and chain leashes flashed by, their hairstyles harsh and their cheekbones high, and I felt I'd finally arrived at the club I'd fantasized about—one of the massive ones fictionalized in movies about underground scenes. E led me around, explaining the different areas and their reputations, noting that whole worlds are created here, in effect. For some, alternate lives are lived out in this space, and those lives have their own highs and lows. That's why, when you ask someone to go to Berghain, the response is often a quick, far-off frown, like they're remembering a dream.

What if there was another version of me living in this fantasy world at a fantasy club with dark, heavy music? This version wouldn't talk or smile, and she'd still dye her hair black. I wished I were younger when I was there, even though a lot of the people there looked older. I wished I'd been going there for years.

Planes are little worlds, with their own economies and living conditions and behavioral norms. The challenge of creating a comfortable space here is much more appetizing to me than, say, camping. By the end of every flight, I'm in a terrible mood, but while it's going on I mostly have hope that I will be able to handle things more efficiently and appear on the other side a better person.

Luxury bestowed on the almost luxury-immune writer isn't well-documented. We're supposed to be embarrassed. In these rare dispatches, the writer is always taken aback, finding the gifts from embassies, festivals, etc. hard to accept. The gifts, though, are to be negotiated, which makes things even more awkward for the writer. She'll take what she gets, thank you. So she gets a terrible flight time and a motel at the edge of town. That's okay; she would like to be left alone. On the last day of her trip, she realizes she had a stipend to spend at the hotel bar that will now go to no one. And what's worse to a broke writer than a bar tab going to waste?

I love perks to a fault. It means I like following rules and being rewarded. I'm appalled when someone with whom I'm dining orders something too specific by making substitutions. I've never sent anything back because I don't want to shoot the messenger, which is the waiter. How are people who learn to act rich—once they are rich—wrung so dry of their guilt?

A flight attendant spilled Coke on my non English-speaking neighbor's white sweater, who silently reached for a napkin from the cart, but the flight attendant, who hadn't noticed the spill, made a barricade with her hand and frowned at the woman, saying, "Do you need something?" as one would to a baby reaching for adult food. Later, the same attendant said into the intercom, "Will whoever just went into the bathroom—unless it's an emergency—please come out?" I was half asleep, having taken a pill, seatbelt fastened, seat back and tray table upright.

* * *

The reason, I read, behind Donald Trump's tweet about a news anchor "bleeding badly from a facelift" was because her news show pointed out that the *Time* magazine covers displayed in several Trump resorts aren't real. The coverage of these types of events sound like someone trying not to laugh.

Independence Day makes me lonely, even though there are fireworks going off around me and it isn't even evening yet. I went out with friends last night and the night before, but it still seems like the city's been deserted. I assume some people are on Fire Island, a place I've never been. It looks nice, but expensive. I love expensive things but I hate being around the people who can afford them.

I'm reading a review of the TV show *Fire Island* by someone who is writing a novel set on Fire Island. In the article, he recounts a mini-protest his house staged with signs that read "literally any other beach" as a reaction to straight couples in a house next door. Since I've never been, when I imagine Fire Island I think of Frank O'Hara getting hit by a jeep there, an island with no roads.

Today I see many memes made from a photo taken of New Jersey Governor Chris Christie at a beach that his state administration closed, enjoying the empty sands with his whole family. There are delicate explosions all around my apartment, punctuating the passing trains on the nearby aboveground track.

* * *

It doesn't seem right to get excited about a piece of journalism that has nothing to do with America's ties to Russia, but this interview with the former fashion director of *Vogue UK* is delicious because it's so tame, and yet it's considered outspoken for the industry. It's the first time I've seen anyone as top tier in fashion magazine world call out the process of pandering to advertisers by placing their clothing on covers.

Maybe this isn't so shocking to most people, but the idea that fashion magazines aren't really saying anything that they want to say about fashion mystified me while I worked at one. Because what was the point, then? The spin other news outlets are giving this controversial interview is that it's about a woman scorned by a (gay) man. She doesn't seem bitter to me, though. Just over it. The newly appointed editor fired her because she was viewed as no longer relevant, but in her words, fashion magazines aren't relevant.

No one who works at a *Vogue* actually reads the magazine. If a fashion writer wants the products she's pushing, she can get them for free, but she's supposed to pretend she can afford them on her tiny little salary. It's a game sustained by pressure alone. The way I was paid and the way I was expected to dress and socialize while editing a fashion magazine were two parallel lines on a chart, never bending or crossing each other. But no one ever talks about that in print. I even heard a lot of people say at parties, "You know you're not supposed to talk about this," about the whole 1:1 ratio of advertising pages to editorial.

Everyone in magazines and in advertising is obsessed with Studio 54. Recreating the feeling of the party, the eclecticism of the guests, the gossip about it on Page Six, the emptiness of an Andy Warhol superstar. It's the basis of basically every fashion campaign ever since. But the people who were really there can't recreate it. There are parties going on all over Brooklyn that are being mined for their diversity and youth instead. The literary brat pack can write about that, if they're around. "How do magazine writers get paid these days?" I asked a man who was interviewing me on a college radio show. I think the older ones all moved to Connecticut or upstate.

Nothing in fashion magazine world makes any sense anymore and maybe it never did. Men always decided what women wear— CEOs, designers (for the advertising brands), photographers, the new editor at *Vogue UK*. Should it not be a given that a woman's opinion is worth more than a man's when it comes to women's fashion? It isn't now and never was. My old editor-in-chief (a man) mostly hired men. At one point I was the only female in the office other than the accountant.

The interviewer thanked me, off the air, for mentioning that older writers don't know how to get paid by magazines anymore. He'd interviewed quite a few and asked them pointed questions about the industry. Apparently, they don't like to admit that it's impossible to have these fabulous New York editorial writing careers anymore, even if they've moved away from New York. Maybe there's still this dream of being one of those writers who lives and works on an island. Maybe they don't want to bite the hand that feeds them, even if it's feeding them about half as much per word as it did in the nineties.

But I'm living that dream, I said. I'm writing a column that's based on a series that Marguerite Duras wrote in 1980. No longer do I have to worry about editing down an article I worked on for weeks to make room for something I vomited up under a pseudonym simply to please an advertiser. "How do you do it?" the interviewer asked. "Simple," I said. "I also work in advertising."

* * *

I didn't have a computer in college. In grad school, I'd take my laptop to the diner or the laundromat, but then it was stolen out of the trunk of my car. I bought another and always left it at home, but that one was stolen while I was on vacation. My first iPhone was stolen out of my hand, by a guy who jumped into a moving car. I have no idea how I could afford to replace any of those things. I hope that there are still computer labs on college campuses.

I'm on the Upper East Side, where it's quiet for New York and the sidewalks are wider. On most buildings, as Marge Simpson once pointed out about a fancier house than her own, the street address is spelled out in cursive. This season on *The Real Housewives of New York City*, one housewife married a notorious cheater for money and has tried tirelessly to create a storyline about finally falling in love. One is trying to move back into the UES because she's totally lost downtown. One's new tagline is "There's nothing gray about my gardens." The two vying for the protagonist position are accusing each other of having failing businesses (which are their personal brands, at this point). The only newcomer is Tinsley Mortimer, who was basically the inspiration for all of these shows, and *Gossip Girl*.

When I talk about the reality show with friends, they seem to miss the surreality of these historically wealthy areas that are mostly now in decline, their outdated sets of rules, and where middle-aged women who were once trophy wives fit into this bubble. Walking here, I watched an older woman walk into the Carlyle, the older doorman making light conversation as he push-started the revolving door's cycle for her. Another woman, in a pink shirtdress and espadrilles, hobbled across Lexington as if much older than she looked. Spotting a friend, she waved both arms in the air, laughing. Everyone is tan and wearing a blonde blowout but I don't feel intimidated by them because they all, even the teenagers, look scared.

Another blonde, tan woman in a pink polo shirt, pink eye shadow, black eyeliner, and a pink gel manicure sitting next to me just opened the door for an old man who simply yelled, "What?" at her. She's loudly gossiping about some big business deals with a younger man sitting across from her. It sounds like his wife works at Amazon. I've been thinking about moving up here because it's actually cheaper than a lot of Brooklyn now. I want to be near Central Park—why not? I don't really care about parks but I do like that one. I'd miss Bed-Stuy, but there, I'm clearly a gentrifier, while here, I could be mistaken for some rich person's adult daughter who has yet to move out.

Nothing here is experimental, except, presumably, the art in all these galleries. One can find a classic wedge salad and a dirty gin martini on every block. People wearing big diamonds and Gucci sunglasses will order a Lipton tea and a plate of mealy sliced tomatoes for lunch. All the dogs could be in a 1950s painting. I'm not so much interested in the character of a Manhattan neighborhood as I'm interested in the people who seem to know all about it. Usually they're awful to talk to and great to eavesdrop on. As the lines become more and more arbitrary, there are types—writers, most of them—who cling to them.

The man and woman next to me are discussing a book about law school called *Getting to Maybe*. I can tell she doesn't want this conversation to end, but she doesn't care about the answers to her own questions. He's just starting law school, and she graduated in 1999. She's talking faster and faster: "You'd be proud of me, I took the subway the other day." She's not talking about being a lawyer, just her memories of law school, the smell of a new notebook. "Like I go to Doctor Herbert for fun? Like I don't have anything else going on—well, I don't have anything else going on."

* * *

My office shares bathrooms with a casting agency. I was at first told by a coworker that it was a modeling agency, but not all of the girls looking at themselves for too long in the mirror are skinny and tall. Some are small children with mothers. Standing beside them, I pretend to cast these people in parts. She could be the bitchy roommate, or the oblivious receptionist, or the winning lawyer (the losing one is always a man), or a new kid in school. None look like stars, but maybe it's the lighting, or maybe I wouldn't be able to recognize a star if I saw one.

I once met a casting agent who scouted for reality TV, and she didn't seem at all like a conniving nihilist. She seemed pretty uninteresting, actually. I've talked with an editor for *The Real Housewives of Atlanta*, who kind of summed up the footage she pieced together when she said, "These women just want nothing to do with one another." It was difficult to get them to agree to interact, even though they were contracted to, and so there was a lot of unusable stuff wherein the stars tried to create their own storylines away from the others.

Reality show stars must be volatile enough to cause drama but complacent enough to play along. It was Donald Trump's job once, to a certain extent, to cast the players on a reality show. According to an interview he did, he's mad that he cast Jeff Sessions as Attorney General in the show he's putting on as President. Maybe it's that easy to win America back. Maybe all they want is the return of the catchphrase, "You're fired."

* * *

Sometimes, depressing shit just piles up and becomes a stack of evenly flat turds. Other times, a large-scale awful thing feels minimized by personal drama. The shit is everywhere but it's gaseous, just in the air. America (the world?) is obsessed with poop humor right now. Based on the poop emoji, there is a cartoon character in a children's movie named Poop; there are poop-shaped birthday cakes; and poop-shaped pool toys float, like real poops do, in pools this summer.

Returning from an upstate wedding, I received a sort of devastating phone call. Suffering a loss is so much more acute than suffering the many burdens with which our horrific government is trying to punish us. A loss is right there on you, a weight that you can't get used to, hot and cold at the same time.

How does one stop from reaching for the phone, when one has to reach for the phone to do everything else? It's been a while since I knew this frustration. At least I know that my book is still being taught in schools since I keep getting Google alerts about it being free to illegally download. But nothing gets easier, ever. Everything gets harder and more sad because it happened again and it's still not over or perfect.

* * *

Music festivals are pretty awful. I've been to a few with press passes. For this one, I got a guest pass. I can't imagine actually paying for a ticket. People with general admission have to wait in long lines to get in or to go inside any of the sponsored tents. They're not allowed in certain secluded areas that have shorter lines for bathrooms and better cocktails to buy.

If I were writing a story on this festival, I'd write that general admission ticketholders are constantly reminded that they could have it better if they'd paid more for VIP access, so they're being advertised to in that way, on top of all the other ads. And I'd write about the American Express tent with a lame Plinko game and a staged selfie op, the Bai tent in VIP with samples and a Polaroid photographer, the Toyota tent with makeovers and a selfie video op in the car, the HP "lab" with a scary play in which the walls close in on the audience and a dome projection that reminded me of being high on cough syrup and watching Pink Floyd laser light shows at the planetarium.

The only thing that seems to have emerged from any of these market research pavilions is a proliferation of branded selfies. Now, even dive bars in Brooklyn have free digital photo booths that provide good lighting and a gif perfect for posting in exchange for your email address. It's comforting to know that even huge, cutting-edge companies are having a hard time moving beyond that.

Even Anthony Scaramucci, who was such a pleasure to read about for those few days he was the White House's communications director, is gone, fired by the new Chief of Staff just after his pregnant wife left him. I hope she becomes a Real Housewife. I hope I become a Real Housewife. I think I used to be a better writer.

I try to sleep and sometimes I can, but other times I lay awake thinking terrible things and then I have to go drink lots of coffee and go to work, even though the atmosphere around my eyes looks like it's crawling. I think that it's not as bad as it could be but that's a really hopeless thought, isn't it? And then I think I'm stupid to have ever thought it was all going to be fine for me. Why me, and basically no one else?

I rejoined my gym. But back when I went before, I listened to hardstyle mixes on Soundcloud for motivation, and now, the stabbing reminder that a lot of the people I know that play this kind of music have gone through a Pepe wormhole and come out the other side an alt-right bro. It turns out that when the conservative party is the edgier one, it attracts much of the fringe, like artists. All that posturing as hackers and vapid party girls sometimes sticks.

I've dragged myself to a treadmill, I've subscribed to a hardstyle podcast, and I've downloaded an hour-long mix. The momentum is working, but there is a voiceover sample getting louder as the beat slows down: a speech by George W. Bush. Maybe it will be part of a joke—he'll say something dumb and there will be an explosion sound effect? But it continues, and the music swells when he talks about God and our country, much in the same way it does when lyrics describe finding the true meaning of life on the dance floor.

I keep coming across these ominous signs that predate Trump's election. When the jokes became real. When borrowing from bigoted cultures led to internalized bigotry. When political correctness became a meme for the youngest millennials. When "fake news" was simply conspiracy theory clickbait like Illuminati codes, and friends reposted it earnestly. Should I have confronted them?

I mostly don't talk to anyone in my circle about sensitive subjects like immigration policies or affirmative action or minority representation in the media because I assume they share my own half-formed opinions. Or that they don't have opinions. Or that their opinions differ from mine only because they're uninformed and I'm not the most informed person either so we may as well not mention any of it. And now it feels like you have to be either on the right side or the wrong side, and a lot of people I assumed would be on one are on the other.

* * *

Is having sex really unpopular now? That's how old I feel. I have no idea if the really sexy people on social media are having real sex or not. Cool if not—but do they think it's cool, or are they sad about it? Cool if they are, too. I don't want to have an opinion about this one because I feel especially uninformed.

Trump would have loved to be young now, constantly dogged by opportunities to self-promote and go on dates using apps. There's a type of tackiness that's acceptable because it was funny and then it became fashionable because it was so left-field. But while that was going on, Trump was normalizing a similar tackiness, as were other reality TV people.

The way the political situation is infiltrating my social life is alarming, because it isn't. What a strange time to be meeting new people and keeping conversation light because that's the protocol. The alternative, I guess, would be to bring up neo-Nazis on a first date. I do love discovering for myself all the new systems my single friends have described. There are different expectations and the pacing has changed. Maybe that's why my heart is racing all the time.

I look at pictures on Instagram of girls taking baths together, taking pictures of themselves in the baths, sprinkling flower petals in the water and doing drugs. It reminds me of the times I spent with my best friend in high school in her room, which were the best times of my life maybe, but the whole time, we were wishing we could get a ride somewhere else in Michigan. Would these girls rather not leave their Brooklyn apartments? There's a train that could take them anywhere if they wanted it to. Is posting the picture better than leaving?

I love to leave. I get to the party early and I stay the whole night, but even as I'm leaving the party because the lights are coming on, people are going to another one, and there are towering drag queens everywhere trying to keep people awake and it looks like a movie about New York, and I say that to my date, whoever he is, and he agrees because he wants to be a part of it, too.

* * *

I wanted to write about seeing Chris Kraus in so many fashion photoshoots lately and wanting to be like her, but I remembered that when I stayed with her in Winnipeg this summer, I'd heard about the Helmut Lang ads and asked her how the shoot went. "This isn't what I wanted, Natasha," she said, laughing. She'll take it, of course, she reasoned.

"What did you want?" I asked.

"A good review in the *New York Review of Books*," she said. She advised I stick with the literary scene I somehow came into contact with in New York. But that's not what I wanted. At least it's not what I want anymore.

I'm angry that I can't not generalize about men anymore, because there have been too many occasions in which heeding generalizations would have served me better than my instinct to trust that everyone is capable of acting outside of the temptations that privileges afford them. But enough about men. But what isn't about men?

I've been accused by a bitter ex, more than once over the years, that I'm not capable of writing about anything other than myself. And that's a gendered accusation only because the feminine confessional style is a cliché. Same ex said I shouldn't move to New York because I'll end up one of those writers writing about New York. Same ex was the first person who encouraged me to publish my novel. It's not about New York or myself, but it could be.

I want to gossip about New York's nonexistent literati. Just that they think they're something and they're not, that kind of thing. That someone I slept with once was judging a debut fiction award and didn't vote for my novel, even though some of the other entries were garbage and we both know it. That all of these people network in sorority-like conditions, over "drinks," which could mean so many things. But if I started talking about them as some kind of literati it would validate something that I think is really not there right now. It's all interns.

I can't stand New York publishing world functions. Everyone is reading some latest book, either because they have to or because they want to impress someone that has to. So everyone is reading something they don't really want to read and then that's how everyone ends up hating everything and saying that there's nothing good out there. That or they're jealous.

* * *

I'm at a place in which I feel I don't deserve to be, trying to grasp the concept of what it is to deserve. I am in a hotel room in Paris having breakfast in bed, switching the TV station from the only English channels, which are reporting on the US border camps set up to retain children who were forcefully separated from their parents as a deterrent for immigration to a radio channel playing classical music. Americans sometimes say they would move to Paris if it weren't for the xenophobic French, but we don't have that excuse anymore. This is my first time here, which surprises everyone I speak to, since I've worked "in fashion industry" for years.

I'm very lucky, I keep thinking and hearing from colleagues, to be writing for fashion houses instead of about them, for magazines. It doesn't seem logical, to think this way, as a writer, but the truth is that somehow, the whole industry has been turned around so that the brands have more freedom than the press, and anyway, fashion is so ephemeral that writing about it concretely is a fool's errand. Making a narrative for—not of—a brand is the space in which a writer can truly be creative. That said, it's paid work. Fashion journalism is paid by magazines, which are paid by brands, whereas copywriting is paid by brands (you do the math). I'm here for money, since all of publishing is corrupt.

Walking back to my hotel after a meeting, I passed a sidewalk café full of people who were clearly here for fashion week and, despite myself, felt sorry for them. They're instantly recognizable, even though I recognized no one: the shoes are this season and the clothing is a little too layered for the hot weather, the fit never quite sexy. As my Midwestern cousin said at my sister's wedding (covered by Vogue.com), "You can tell the New York people from the Michigan or Arizona or Connecticut people because the New York people's clothes are either too big or too small, and everyone else is just wearing something that fits."

How can anyone say that the money they should be getting paid should be enough to buy Manhattan property? One might as well ask to buy an island, I think. But this, I'm told, is a problem I have with the concept of what it is to deserve. One deserves what one can confidently ask for. One deserves everything if she can be everything for someone else. It doesn't really matter how productive one is, as long as she never lets the company down. It's about a presence. Or sometimes it's clout.

"Do you feel like an imposter?" my therapist asked me. "I'm aware of the syndrome," I said. I often wonder if she hates me. On the (business class) red-eye over here, I had a dream that she finally told me she did, and all the reasons why.

My computer sometimes synchs to my text messages automatically, and so a backlog of a few days appears in succession in the upper right hand corner of the screen. A man I'm enamored with at the moment tells me, in two seconds, that he misses me, that he's proud of me, that he is having a hard time at work, that he can't go on like this, not sleeping enough between jobs, that my last day in town was a dent in his schedule he's now regretting.

I'm now regretting sending him a picture of my tray of French pastries and sliced kiwi fruit with an ornately latticed balcony just beyond it. I always do this. I insist that men should be impressed by me until they are, and then they can't stand it. I would hate it if I were them, too. I imagine, sometimes immediately after I say something or send something, that it will be the thing they repeat to their friends when asked why we broke up. She was so self involved, he'll say. Can you believe she sent me this text? He'll hold it up and they'll laugh and roll their eyes together, knowing that no woman in her early 30s can survive the coming years with a head that big. "You deserve everything," he'll say, for now.

I'm looking at the cover of *Forbes* that predicts Kylie Jenner to be the world's youngest "self-made" billionaire based on her passion for "beauty" and thinking "self-made" seems pretty relative in this context and also that she must have to convince herself that she deserves this title. An impossible feat, I'd think. She and her family must repeat the words "worked really hard for this" to one another a lot. Have I worked really hard for anything? It's entirely up to me to decide what "really hard" could mean.

* * *

Someone told me that I should write a book about jealous writers, since I'm so invested in the subject. It's true: I try to justify it, hoping to appear introspective about the idea of jealousy, instead of simply unhealthily jealous myself.

I have a rival, a writer I've never met, and the origin of our rivalry can be traced back a decade. She's my favorite one to be jealous of because she was once less successful than I was and now she's likely surpassed me, in terms of this silly literary status game that only we can see. I've only spoken to her once on the phone, ten years ago, but since then she's inspired me, and I know I've inspired her, since I'm mentioned in an essay in her new book.

Reading that essay was one of the most surreal experiences of my life. In short, this writer—this rival—cleared up a lot of what had been worrying me for all these years in just a few phrases. From her prose style, I could tell that she'd never confront me directly about it. Instead, she saves everything for the page. Everything has to hang in the balance of her literary devices. While hearing this portrayal of me and of the events that led to our rivalry, I was shocked, and then hurt, and then resentful, and then strangely self-satisfied. (She couldn't quite help herself, could she? Me neither, clearly.)

From the internet, I know that she and I have much in common. I want to make a long list of the similarities, starting with her teenage love for certain films and ending with men she's loved and agents she's employed. I know that if we weren't so similar, it wouldn't matter how successful she was. I could be jealous of plenty of writers. Plenty, even, who have been linked romantically to my exes. Either they don't seem worthy or they came too late, though.

And yet she's nothing like me. We have different tastes, different agendas, different friends. No one gets why I pay her any attention, other than my therapist, who has the benefit of seeing only the story, not the real life scenery. She often brings up my need for narrative, but about my rival writing an essay about me, "You can't make this stuff up," she says.

Someone sent me a clip montage from movies in which characters say, "We're not so very different, you and I." Usually it was a villain to his foe, the hero. A loaded throwaway line. My sister is my twin, and sometimes we say to each other, slowly, "the same…but different." It's from a movie, but I forget which one.

I'm jealous of girls who look enough like me but have better figures and prettier faces than I do, and that these girls are usually younger doesn't comfort me at all. So many people must be jealous of me, my sister says, at the fancy party we're invited to. My jealousy should diminish, but it doesn't, and I think that's the nature of it. Or that's the nature of me.

* * *

In an interview, I was asked to describe the best party I can remember attending. I went to a record label's 21st anniversary party at the Palms in Las Vegas in 2010. Almost every artist on the roster performed at the theater there over the course of three days. I must have driven up to Vegas alone, through the flat desert, over the Hoover Dam, and onto the strip.

I was invited by a band I'd roadied for. The room we shared was on, like, the 20th floor. I can still remember the gray light coming in through a huge window overlooking that hot, crawling city. In the hotel, we ran into old rockers in the elevator, saw the younger ones freak out, did drugs in the rooms, drank Bloody Marys by the pool, gambled, won.

When I drove home, I hit torrential rain so strong I couldn't see ahead of me on these winding mountain roads. As I told this story to the interviewer, I said that the whole experience, looking back, felt metaphorical, as stupid as that sounds. I was about to move to New York, so it was the end of me going to school or touring with bands or partying for days. I'd broken up with someone, too. And the storm was like that part of a movie that flips everything, like the wedding scene in Robert Altman's *Dr. T and the Women*.

When the article was published, all the details were left out: the names of the bands that played, what drugs I did, the guys who invited me. The party sounded like a generic Vegas weekend, which I guess is cool, too.

* * *

I'm pretty sure I have pink eye. Before I moved to New York eight years ago, I used to call my sister here every day at the same time and talk to her while she rode the train home from work. I remember laughing at her for getting pink eye. She was defensive about it, saying that all day in New York, we touch disgusting things like the metal poles in the train cars that sometimes look like a braid of hands. There are many kinds of pink eye, I'm reading, and most of them just go away on their own, after a few weeks of oozing like a squinting alley cat, but they're all "extremely contagious."

New York is a cesspool. My first reaction to most of the places I've been outside America is "It's so clean." Some people say they love the griminess of New York, but I think that what I love can be described as an attitude. Maybe the griminess and the attitude are inextricably linked. Maybe the way this city is built, with too many competing public transit systems and not enough recycling bins and hot garbage air blowing up from the sidewalks, is its true essence.

Maybe that Manhattan is surrounded by dirty rivers teaming with barges full of waste, overflowing dumps in New Jersey, Sanitation's finest in Staten Island, and Brooklyn's gasoline-scented Coney Island ocean waves is what props it up as this gleaming thing, this diamond in the trash. Maybe I'm just annoyed because every time I feel like I've reached a higher level of living here, the city's hot dirty hands poke me in the eye. This summer has been particularly hot and cold, literally.

I said I'd never write about my trips to Staten Island because they were too precious to me, too close to something that could have been real, whatever that means. In fact, I was lost in some dream of what my reality is, after the rug was pulled out from under me in so many ways (a stagnant long-term relationship that turned out to be a lie, among other things).

After a few comically bad dates to get back on my feet, I told a garbage man to meet me at a bar in Ridgewood. It was another novelty, something to tell my friends the next time we got together for margaritas after work. But then I saw him, his strong features and long eyelashes, and I heard his Staten accent make jokes about literature that were smart, but at half-speed, punctuated too often with "like," like some mob movie sidekick. He was one of the characters that the movie star I used to date played, but for real.

We both smoked but had started out wanting to hide that from the other. When we went out for a cigarette, he pointed out his $800 junker with red dice on the rearview. He didn't understand why people moved to New York, still, and I said I wasn't sure, either. Why did I move here? It wasn't because I felt more alive here, like I could see electricity in the streets. That was the first time I made him laugh.

Most Staten Islanders can't imagine moving to Manhattan because of this thing that happens when you're so close but so far away, this proximity that feels like a wall instead of water: when you grow up right there but never really there, it feels like the place is off-limits. It's easier to get to Manhattan from Arizona, for example, than it is from Staten Island, because you're oblivious to certain things about it.

So close, but so far away, I repeated. His route was Chinatown, one of the most notoriously garbage-strewn parts of New York. I told him he may as well have said he was a cowboy, I found the trucks so romantic.

I thought for sure he could see through me and my privileged fascination with his industry and his outsider/New Yorker status, but he offered me a ride home and then had this little speech planned once we parked: he'd like to see me again, but understood I probably wasn't interested—it was nice, though, the conversation that seemed to last a few minutes and was actually three hours. I looked at him, and it had been so long since I'd seen someone in that seat other than a cab driver.

Of course we kissed, for a long time, and it wasn't perfect but it was a nice kiss because neither one of us thought it would happen, we were each so insecure about the other person's set of issues with the way the date could be read. No matter what way it would go, it was just this really nice thing already.

* * *

It didn't work out between the garbage man and I, I guess because I'm self-involved. I remember being in the passenger's seat of his car, my shins propped on his dash, going on about my feelings on plastic surgery, having sort of an existential crisis trying to accept its role in modern post-op society while keeping a healthy skepticism of obsessives, when he reached over me to roll down my window and hand a dollar to a young homeless woman standing on a median.

Once, he insisted on coming to a reading I was doing at MoMA PS1 when he found out he had just enough time to drive up to Long Island City before he'd have to circle back to Chinatown for work. He had never heard of PS1, but that didn't mean he had never seen performance art or developed a hilarious cynicism towards it. Staten Island was far away in so many respects, and close in so many others.

While we wandered the museum, acquaintances kept stopping me to say that they had missed my reading because they couldn't find it. I kept smiling and saying that this was totally ideal because I hate doing readings but I love getting attention. I tried to see the place from his perspective, but couldn't: I thought it would be the fashion week-level styling and rainbow of unnatural hair colors that would throw him (to me, PS1 always looks like a movie set cast for a '90s club scene but during the day and outdoors, like a self-aware portrait of the Limelight emptying out in the morning), but he didn't seem affected by that. It was my comfort-level around this sheer amount of people that intimidated him.

When we left, he said he saw a few people buying my book from the store. "Every penny counts," I said, reminding him that sales are almost meaningless to an author unless they're in the millions. It was this game I kept playing, letting him know that he should be impressed by me and then letting him know that I considered my own success negligible, which probably made him feel like nothing.

On Valentine's Day, he was working. I wasn't sad at all, didn't need flowers or a date. In fact, I was so used to guys intentionally forgetting the holiday, I was elated when I got a text that morning wishing me a happy one. And then I got a text that asked me my current location, since I happened to be in the Lower East Side, another saying to come outside and down the street. It was a foggy night and I was near the Manhattan Bridge and I could see the huge parked truck backlit by it but obscured by the atmosphere. On the other corner was the garbage man in uniform, alone because he'd been assigned the dump that day, which meant he hauled a load to New Jersey, without a partner. He apologized for being dirty, even dirtier than usual. There were always undercover patrolmen watching the garbage trucks, he informed me, and so he had to get back to work. He'd just wanted to say Happy Valentine's Day in person.

Within the New York Department of Sanitation, there were many, many rules, but garbage truck drivers could basically ignore traffic laws. He dreamed of getting off of his 18-month beginner's probation and using one of his three strikes to sideswipe a car cutting him off on the Turnpike, for example. "Think about it. You wanna play chicken with a garbage truck?" We broke up just before his probation ended and he took his first vacation in years. I don't know where he went for it, if he even left.

I had a dream about him later, and in it, he had become a performance artist with a painted face—the type of person he said he couldn't stand. I could tell I was being tested: did I like him enough to stand by him while he did a lot of loud, embarrassing things at a place I considered cool? What if he brought all his dumb friends with him and barely paid attention to me? What if he wasn't actually a garbage man?

"This isn't some Lady and the Tramp kind of thing," I calmly argued when I got the breakup phone call from him ("he dumped me like it was his goddamn job," I say to friends now that I'm over it). "I live with four roommates in Brooklyn and grew up on welfare." We had quit smoking together on New Year's Day and it was February twenty-something. His laugh was still hoarse and probably always would be. "Uptown Girl," he joked.

"Just a little up and over," I said, and then, because it wasn't a joke, "Well I'm going to be devastated." He sounded surprised. "You won't be, though. I mean you shouldn't be." He sounded so practical, so measured, I had to make an outrageous demand. "I can never talk to you again." That got him. I reasoned that if our problem as a couple had been the long distance, being friends surely wouldn't work. He had to see the logic there.

Of course we talked again, but eventually decided I was right, even though I hadn't wanted to be. It's better to keep him as a memory on a distant island rather than a texting friend who reveals more or less of the things I found so endearing about him over time. Whenever I see a garbage truck in Chinatown, I look at the driver and the loader hanging off the back, and I've never seen him.

* * *

Going to the gym is in itself a strange concept, like running on a wheel, but what's worse is that there are too many gyms now; their presence is becoming a burden. Instead of a nice old deli you never went to (but maybe would have) getting torn down for a new Sweetgreen or Starbucks, it's being torn down for a SoulCycle, old people complain.

And of course we should all go, but it's the talking about going that bothers us. Describing one's fitness and beauty routine is the most boring flirtation. It's describing a method of looking better, which suggests you think you look good, and also that you don't think you look good enough. It's usually a comparison of activities and goals, a display of both arrogance and desperation. I always interrupt conversations about workouts to ask if one would be just as inclined to describe the amount of Botox one gets, and then detail the process.

But it's such a common conversation, and it shouldn't be shameful, since, you know, the health part. Plus it's a way people meet each other. Dating profiles are often all about extreme fitness and looking for partners who share those interests. Looking at my friends' gay hookup apps, half the selfies are in gyms, and many more are on mountain hikes (the rest are in tiny bathroom or fitting room mirrors). But if what you're working towards is, primarily, a sexy physique, then wouldn't you assume it would be sexier if you made the steps you're taking a secret?

I'm not saying anything should be hidden because it's ugly, just that the concept of broadcasting a need for acceptance so strong it requires hours of struggle seems inherently unattractive. This question is more about what constitutes sexiness now, seeing as most of the ideal-shaped celebrities shrink their waists using Photoshop before posting a paparazzi or runway picture on Instagram (there's proof: I follow a private account that makes before-and-after gifs of famous people photos found on Getty or Vogue and their own filtered, finessed versions). I have the same mini existential crisis when I hear a celebrity say, "I've always been passionate about makeup."

Makeup, as a thing to be passionate about, outwardly. A conversation about a way to look enhanced. Admitting this: not only that the pressure from a misogynistic and image-obsessed society has flattened you (it has, come on), but that you'd rather become a spokesperson for image alteration than to be called a phoney.

We respect shape-shifters. That's easy to understand: Madonna-level transformations, drag queen contouring, costumes of any kind are welcome escapes from the self. It's fun to watch performers do it, and it's fun to do it ourselves, to see what it's like to get a different type of attention. I'm just amazed that so many people go out as someone else in search of anonymous sex, when all of that stuff comes off on a pillow. Have you ever seen the brownish skull shape a lot of makeup makes, when one falls asleep before washing her face? It's the best when there are false eyelashes stuck somewhere, too, cross-eyed and smirking little mask.

The more we're accepting of progressive ideas about identification, of course, the more I have to be okay with any decision a woman makes about carving out her shoulder fat in a photo she posts for her millions of insecure fans. You gain some, you lose some.

I'm getting into dangerous territory, maybe. I just wish my friends liked that they're aging, and that I didn't have this fear about very young people trying to stay home so that a bigger audience could appreciate a more constructed image. I know they must be thinking that what their physical high school classmates think of their physical bodies will never matter. The truth is, it does. Those brats will expose your secrets for no apparent reason.

Just after writing this, I happened to read a post about a male model commenting on Kim Kardashian's Instagram account that "She's not real," and that her surgeon "fucked up" one of her hips. For context, this was on an image from a time when Kim went on a talk show and said she doesn't have anything bad to say about Donald Trump. Kim's reply to the model was, "Sis we all know why you don't care for it," which implies that he's gay if he's not attracted to her (he's not gay). The model's response was, "My opinion on plastic surgery stays the same, not for me! I personally don't care for it! Done end of story!"

My first thought was that it's nice to see a straight man attack her for creating an unrealistic image, which I guess is a pretty vicious way to feel. My next thought was: What would have changed if Kim's comment had been, "Cis we all know why you don't care for it," opening up a conversation about her body modifications in the context of transitioning. It wouldn't fly, but it's where my mind went: we're all transitioning into some avatar of our own creation, anyway. None of this is real, so calling her "not real" seems beside the point. Still, she didn't say cis, she said sis, which is stupid.

The more I think about it, the more I understand that the body trend for the twenty-teens is "in transition," or "work in progress," which totally makes sense for a lot of reasons. And I have to admit that if everyone was altering their physical selves in secret, I'd probably be more upset. Meaning, it's better than the alternative that people addicted to public validation are more inclined to show their work, and because of that we know how impossible certain beauty goals are without so much money.

More importantly, it's heartbreakingly fantastic that non-binary and transitioning identities have a way to find community, and this fact outweighs the outcomes of body shaming forums, I suspect. I mean, obviously the real problem with unattainable beauty standards is that they're rooted in gender constructs imagined by white people millenniums ago. So now, maybe we as a society are accepting the step of slicing everyone up to see if we can create a new set of expectations.

* * *

There's this phobia I have that has nothing to do with technology or the post-truth era or identity politics or that annoying term, "body confidence" or another, "extreme self care." I'm scared of injections. Not necessarily needles themselves, since I can watch a tattoo get drawn, but seeing varicose veins or a tick burrowing into the skin makes me lightheaded. If someone suggests I get a B-12 shot for my hangover, I'm done.

I'm walking around in fear of running into imagery that could make me faint: a storefront suggesting treatments for your spider-webbed legs, a PSA about Lyme disease, a junkie shooting up, insurance ads that are supposed to be comforting but include imagery of IVs. I can't believe I could even write any of that just now. I try to never talk about this phobia, since people tend to roll their eyes about it and then describe a time when a doctor couldn't find a vein when they had to get blood drawn and I have to leave the room and put my head between my knees.

It's another reason why I can't talk about health in general for too long. The conversation is a reminder that I'll one day have to confront my own deficiencies in ways I find horrifyingly invasive. How, if we are we all just sacks of fluid, am I afraid of my own? "Wouldn't you just love to transfer into an artificial body?" asked a friend, on the topic of the pressure to keep up with a body trend, like you owe it to the culture or something. But becoming part AI was the opposite of my point, I thought—that we're all too obsessed with looking artificial. "So," he asked, "you want to live in a human body forever?"

I guess I don't, no. I hate my human body, all of its blemishes and reactions, that I have to protect it from so much and feed it and poke into it with tools of torture, and that candy isn't actually food, it's a non-thing, an ad for itself, but I eat it. We were eating burritos from a truck on a stoop in the West Village, a block away from his apartment and across the street from Anna Wintour's. Richard Gere used to live in this building, too, he said, and on the roof was some shrine for the Dalai Lama.

* * *

What is the best compliment a total stranger could ever give you? If you were rich, would you want the world to know it? For your birthday party, would you rather go to the tastiest restaurant, or the fanciest?

There are people, apparently, who fetishize giving away money to other people who demand it semi-anonymously. This is evidenced by a large number of sexy (often faceless) selfie posts that use hashtags like "cashdrain" and "paypig" and "walletrape" and all these other ones (usually some foot fetish mentions, too), and are captioned with something bossy like "No broke losers, pay piggies wanted." There is no promise of mutual benefit, like with certain live cam sites. There is not a financial goal that will unlock another screen, another image, another live sex act. It's called financial domination (other hashtags are "findom" and "finsub").

I like the term "walletrinse" most, like it's somehow cleansing to pay a stranger for no real reason. Sometimes I, too, get confused about money and it accidentally feels cleansing to spend it, until it's gone, and then I remember that money doesn't work that way. Do these finsub people regret the payments? If they do, is that a regret based in shame, or do they feel duped?

Do the "cash drainers" feel as turned on by payments as the "pay pigs" do? Money is an aphrodisiac, obviously. At a nice restaurant, I noticed that at every table sat an older or very old man and a younger or very young woman. The women were beautiful, with styled hair and highlighted cheeks. The dinner was expensive, the view was almost breathtaking, and all around me girls pulled the ribbons from paper shopping bags containing the gifts that would keep an affair alive.

Someone asked me how much financial status and relative success matter to me in a partner, like he was testing me. Of course I'd like to say that they don't at all, but that's kind of like saying the person's existence doesn't matter. Everyone has a financial status, and I suppose it matters that a person is not staggeringly insecure about his or her own.

Does relative success mean relatively successful (all success is relative) or as successful as me? Success, measured financially? I hardly ever date people with social media accounts, so the numerical value of their popularity hasn't usually come into play. If we're talking about success as in self-satisfaction, I'm not interested. All I really care about is conversation and sex. I would care, then, if the notions of one's net worth or career track inhibited them. That's the most judicious answer I can come up with.

So often, I wonder how people get the money they must have in order to live in New York. People are good about keeping it a secret, but I am not. I will tell you how much I have in my bank account and how much I spend every day, what different clients pay me, and my rates per word for articles. I will tell you a breakdown of my taxes, the day I have to pay them, and then I'll immediately forget.

I try not to talk too much about numbers, because those same people who keep their finances super secret, I've noticed, will tell me that I'm doing everything wrong. I should make myself a business, I should expense everything, I should hire an accountant, I should not have signed a contract. And then from them, on their own fees and budgets: nothing. They sublet their apartments sometimes, but I know that can't be the only source. It's best not to think about it, since the answer is always anti-climactic—it's family money, in so many words.

The fantasy of a sugar daddy is one that we all now know takes a lot of work, and ruins a reputation. That's not the only thing stopping women from courting the relationship, though. It's that there aren't so many to go around, and the rich men know it. An aging sugar baby is in serious danger of being dropped for someone younger. If they married you, you are still getting the axe, sorry. You just went one higher and became a trophy wife, but those are meant to be collected.

The motivation for becoming a sugar baby shouldn't be that it's easy, since it's really not. Fighting natural inclinations in order to appease a phoney agreement is more taxing than waiting on tables, since it doesn't have as many breaks. But getting paid to be sexy is a fetish, just like paying someone sexy is. The motivation ideally, is the fetish, on both ends. There is power in receiving money and there is power in giving it. Both exchanges, when sexual desire is involved, are taboo, but for some reason one is seen as submissive power while the other is understood to be dominating. The designations feel arbitrary at best.

The exchange of money has always been intrinsically related to desire, and therefore it has always been peripheral to sex. I love the idea of turning the actual bank account into a sex organ, asking for it to be filled or emptied, and the additional distance created by blind messages and conflicting hashtags ("findom" and "finsub" are always listed one after the other). Does financial status and success matter to you in a partner? No, say the cashdrainers. What matters is that there is no partner, only the money itself, an extension of no one, an expression of nothing, only a representation of pure desire entering another.

* * *

I never rely on the kindness of strangers. I assume, for the most part, that everyone is trying to get something out of me—me, the one with so little to give. I'm cynical because of what I study (marketing, celebrity, influence, etc., ugh) but also I study what I do because I'm cynical. In my daily life, I see mostly bad behavior. It's my fault, though. I'm lazy and look at what's shown to me, which is a lot of trash, stupidity, and attention seeking (not that I haven't displayed the same behaviors myself, likely more so the more I consume them). The exemplary behaviors are less noticeable, since modesty is essential to that equation.

On Monday, I took a red eye from Newark to Reykjavik to Edinburgh, and then a cab to Glasgow to stay at a friend's apartment during a nine-hour layover. A wasn't home, but his roommate was made aware of my arrival and had coffee and croissants waiting. After a shower, she took me to her favorite charity shops, a classic lunch spot, a cute junk store in an alleyway, and a beautiful park. My body tingled with jet lag but I could tell that my relative silence was not being judged. The sky was a perfect gray marble.

Back at the apartment, she'd arranged a ride back to the airport for me. On time, another stranger drove me the 45-minute distance in exchange for the cost of gas. Sheep and cows and shaggy horses dotted the rolling hills, all of them almost regal in comparison to American livestock. They looked softer and thicker, moving in graceful slow motion.

I kept looking for the catch. Did either woman want to know more about living in New York? "I could never," said the Scottish native. "I've noticed something about people who live there," said the Russian. "They have a way of always needing to hold your attention." My work? "A said I should interview you, but I can't understand what he meant by that," said the artist (she did anyway, about whatever I've been thinking about lately). "I'm sure you could write a movie if you tried it," said the makeup artist, who didn't even know A. I have a bound copy of the artist's dissertation to read on my way back from Europe.

Later that day, in Palma, Mallorca, I was picked up by C on a rented scooter and driven the hour-long distance through mountains to a friend's cliff-side house. I always learn, from hanging out with C, what doing favors for people can do for you—a favor that costs you nothing but means more than money to someone will generally result in the inverse later on. I'm not religious, but sometimes I wish religion worked: that everyone was so charitable, because they had to be.

Instead, I'm so used to being taken advantage of, I can't believe when someone I've never met goes out of their way to make sure I'm comfortable.

Throughout my trip so far, I've had to block messages from a stranger who feels I owe him something and has tried multiple outlets to let me know it. This is a more familiar exchange to me. No, I am not for sale, I insist, I owe you nothing, I told you. And then I get ahead of myself, wanting to know why it seems like I could have been, or wanted to be. What have I done that made you think I was a whore? Oh, that? What was the original question, again?

I can hear the gentle waves from my window. There are no bugs and it isn't humid or too hot, but I'm still in a bikini from when I went snorkeling in the cove and laid out on the rocks smoking rolled cigarettes and drinking lemon soda that tasted better because of the sea salt on my mouth while watching other people jump off of our cliff. The fish restaurant overlooks the water on the other side. Our house is pictured on a postcard we found in town, the only building in the photo.

The books in this house are all the classic novels I've always wanted to read and the food in the refrigerator are all my favorite snacks. It's like when, as a kid, you'd describe the hypothetical best day to your friend, asking if they would rather live that every day forever or go on just one single date with their crush.

You have to choose just one, we'd say, the subtext being that if you didn't choose the date, you didn't love him like you said you did, which means you were not an adult, capable of romantic love. Logically, the crush would have to disappoint you in some way, seeing as there would not be another date.

I still don't know the answer to this ultimatum, I guess. I want to believe people are good, since so many are. I want to go on the perfect date with my crush and live it again every day forever. I want to be a good person, to which good things like this happen, and I don't want you to be jealous of me or feel like I owe you something more than what I can give because I want you to love me like I love you and be happy like I am.

* * *

When I was a teenager, probably right after my mom died, the man who took my virginity came over to my house and sat at the foot of my bed while I fell asleep, playing Iggy Pop's "Passenger" on his guitar. I don't remember a lot from that time period, but I remember a time when I was riding in a car with a bunch of these guys and Billy Idol's "Sweet Sixteen" came on and they laughed and said it was for him, the guy I was with, because he was in his twenties and I was sixteen.

The song wasn't for me, I remember, but for the guy who was carting a teenager along for the ride, sticking me in the backseat with strangers without introducing us. I tried to not talk to anyone and to not let the cherry of my cigarette get too close to the window on the highway, but I would always fuck something up and everyone would laugh incredulously, like, who is this person, and, is this just how stupid someone her age is?

"Passenger," when he played it, wasn't for me, either; it was for himself. He was never the leader of that group, or any group probably, and he was always in the passenger seat or playing bass next to the lead singer or sleeping on the couch or dating a girl who went to a conservative suburban high school without a clue, her hair an awful accidental bleached orange. Maybe I wouldn't even remember this much if it weren't for the virginity thing.

I was trying to drive, then, though: I stole my mom's car when she was out or asleep sometimes, before I had my license. I was a bad driver. I totaled that car, and drove the next into the ground, after breaking off the side rearview and a tail light (my sister and I were dating roommates who lived in an apartment above a record store and a music venue, the parking lot to which was always dusted with broken glass that flattened all of our tires). I hate to drive, still, and the longer it's been since I've parallel-parked or merged across four lanes, the more impossible it seems that I would ever be able to.

You might know that my favorite place to be is on the back of a motorcycle. I am terrified of the way it limits communication, the way weight affects speed and balance but in ways too subtle to bother describing before getting on, the way every little bump is felt and every little spasm is read as discomfort but it usually ends up being ignored by the driver, who is shifting around without realizing how much of his body is being used to control this big thing cutting through air on mountain highways that dip around edges of cliffs with no fences, just chicken wire as warning.

I love the thrill of this ride like I love roller coasters, but I also love the aspect of the unknown, for example the not knowing if I will die. I can't tell how experienced a driver is with his surroundings, but I have to put all my trust into him and tilt my body towards the road slightly when he hugs turns even if it's instinctive to tilt my body up, righting a thing that feels it could topple.

Sometimes phrases repeat in my head to the sound of the wind whipping around my helmet, accidentally turning into a mantra: I want to die, I want to die, I want to die. I don't actually want to die, and nothing about the ride offends me, but I start to picture every way of dying here on this cliff or this busy highway and it seems easier to want to die like this than to be afraid of it. If we get hit or fall, I don't want to live. I'm wearing a bikini and sandals and a helmet. We end up behind a group of bikers that is maybe one hundred strong, all of them wearing brightly colored protective gear. Their bikes are faster than ours, but a fall on asphalt is a fall on asphalt, and people die every year taking selfies on these cliffs, our host tells us.

I never plan trips, only take them. This summer, as a recap, I've been taken to Lima as an assistant, stayed in Provincetown at a friend's AirBnB after being driven up in another friend's rental, ridden in the back of yet another rental upstate, been flown to Paris and put up at a hotel there for work, stayed in a friend's house-sit in Cala Deía, Mallorca, and slept in same friend's friend's guest room in Valldemossa, Mallorca, riding on the back of his rented scooter everywhere. Yesterday, our host drove us in her car to a part of the island she'd never been, where we snorkeled on mushrooms and had to hitchhike back to the parking lot because we missed the last bus.

I'd always rather let someone else decide what I'm doing when it comes to stuff like that, seeing as the planning of something puts a stress on the whole thing that seems counter to what a vacation should be. But if no one planned it and no one could drive I wouldn't go anywhere. "I am a passenger. I ride and I ride." It's terrifying. I could die at any time and it would be stupid, the way I'd let it happen. From the backseat of the stick shift car I watched the sunset, a soft pink line separating the turquoise water and the turquoise sky, disappear behind rocky peaks and silhouetted pines, and then the port below us was lit up, a tiny city of apartments and boats.

Music swelled and passing headlights glared on my greasy window, reflections and flares sparkling like stars below a sky slowly populating with stars. I like that in Iggy Pop's version, it starts out singular ("I am a passenger, I stay under glass, I look through my window so bright, I see the stars come out tonight") but it ends up plural, meaning it's not lonely, being out of control: "Get into the car, we'll be the passenger, we'll ride through the city tonight, see the city's ripped backsides, we'll see the bright and hollow sky, we'll see the stars that shine so bright, the sky was made for us tonight."

After all of this natural beauty and letting life happen to me, the bigness of nature and all of that, I'm ready to go back to New York and ride the subway, experience again the tension of train delays and the closeness of my real life, the one I've had a hand in creating, whether I set out to or not. I'll ride to Palma tomorrow morning, where the airport is, and spend many hours relying on strangers to move out of my way and leave me alone with my thoughts that swarm back over me as the city approaches. I want to die, I want to die, I want to die.

Naming Names

A new magazine created entirely by women was being launched and every article in it was about a woman or things that women would appreciate. All the subjects were the B-listers publicists loved to promote, the ones who liked to be interviewed, the ones who had the time. None of the editors were people I'd worked with, so I didn't know who they were. When I thought about it, most magazines were already run by women and about women anyway.

I took a car to the launch party from my office because I was running late. I was relieved to be alone for ten minutes, smelling of my free Forbidden Euphoria sample. The party was for women only, no plus ones.

A smiling publicist with an iPad checked me in at the door and ushered me up an elevator. Another woman joined me there and smiled. "Are you a member?" she asked.

I'd forgotten I was entering a club. "I'm not, are you?"

"No, but I wish I was. Isn't it great here?"

We were supposed to be celebrating the exclusion of male voices in the classic setting of conspiracy. When we entered the room designated for the dinner, conflicting messages papered a reception pedestal: a copy of the first issue of the magazine was available, as was a brochure about joining the club, and a press packet about a new fragrance called Beau. The fragrance was the sponsor of the party, and so the room had been renovated to reflect its branding.

Glass bottles—an abstracted form recognizable as a male and a female torso embracing, in miniature—stood on the tables as centerpieces.

A group of women I knew peripherally from art and literary events were dressed in matching designer outfits that the sponsor had paid them to wear. I said hello and nervously followed them to another room set up for hair and makeup, only to realize that it was reserved for the outfitted influencers only. I could wait in line for a "light touch up" if I wanted, outside. The girls spread out on a shearling rug and took pictures of one another, laughing about the commodification of feminism they were participating in.

"Women are so trendy right now," one said, describing a pink-covered collection of essays written by women, to which she'd contributed. They had to have seen me standing just outside the room, but when I walked away, no one said anything.

At the club entrance again, a DJ I had met once years ago talked to me, to my surprise. She asked why any of us were there and what this was about. I had no idea, I said. "No offense, but why does the this super-gendered magazine have a gender non-conforming person on the cover?"

We were called to find our name cards at a seated dinner. An all-female staff wearing tuxedos gathered around each table and readied the offerings with oversized utensils. At the nod of a head, the synchronized staff gently dropped the components of our meals on wide white plates.

I listened while a writer, an editor, and a filmmaker discussed what kinds of dogs do well in the city and the best preschools on the Upper East Side. I heard that one preschool was for "absolute delinquents." I heard that some socialite couple I'd never heard of had started an open relationship just after getting married.

I finished my meal quickly and left alone, relieved to enter the cold air outside. Like deep breaths, I inserted my headphones and lit a cigarette. The Manhattan lights at night looked far away as I walked, like this wasn't my city.

I regularly listened to the podcasts of several acquaintances, although I hated my reactions to them. By their nature, one can't agree with everything said on a podcast, and so I felt like I was listening in on a conversation in which I couldn't participate. And then all of my friends asked me if I listened to one or the other, and their reactions seemed so uncomplicated: it's so bad, or it's so good. Everyone was trying to be controversial again, and I didn't want to discourage that, by any means.

Besides, I couldn't throw any stones: my friend's book was finally being released, the one I'd written an afterword for, the one with Abuse in the title, at not the best time. I understood why some people just couldn't talk about certain things now.

I had written some autofiction and submitted it to a magazine that only published it after cutting something that was apparently too pointed. This is what it said:

"I used to think that my ex's position at such an esteemed and intellectual magazine said something about him, something I was supposed to like. Now it was clear, though, that the part of him that participated in the magazine—its pretentious parties hosted at a perverted old man's mansion with the same white swing band and the same buffet meal and the same rumors about a coke-fueled S&M party starting at 3am, its fancy dinners that always chose one token ethnic person to award among the old standbys and hot writers, its ridiculous editor who never asked me about my writing but instead told me how great my boyfriend was, and who apparently had angered plenty of young female writers by coming on to them or worse—was the part I hated most about him."

Said editor left the magazine shortly after I wrote that part, before the piece was published (without it). Legally, I was told, I couldn't include it, but that meant politically, since all the other things in there were just as bad. If I had a podcast, it would be a disaster. Even the art I like becomes the art I hate, or vice versa. I felt really in love with my boyfriend when, weeks after a long drunk speech about the Ramones actually truly sucking, he put on a Ramones song while getting dressed in his room and said, "What was I thinking? The Ramones are so good, I love them so much."

I looked at a series of verified Instagram posts about a corporation's efforts to educate and become educated about digital sustainability. Videos asked tech-preneurs, students, and professors what digital sustainability was, and, like a parody show, they all came up with a paper-thin answer at odds with the one before it. We must keep abreast of new solutions, find the best way to adapt to shifts occurring everywhere, make sure to eliminate the excessive and recycle the emergent. Mine young minds. The secret sauce. Innovation where you least expect it. All of the comments were enthusiastic and kind, congratulating the brand for trying to think differently for once.

I listened as podcasters described the political state as a tone being played continuously, its pitch getting higher, with no sign of a drop. They described worshipping chaos in these troubled times. They described a world in which everyone is a corporation, the inverse or neoliberal version of "corporations are people."

I watched a lecture about how the earth's surface has been crusted by a layer of design, that boundaries of every type are mutable, since they are man-made. I watched another about scarcity becoming less desirable in the area of luxury, and what that could mean for consumerism.

Everything I watch and listen to is coming from a person using a platform to sell a product. They sell art, tote bags, and T-shirts that come in vinyl bags. But more than that they're all selling themselves, and I am too, and I hate myself for it, but even more I hate that I believe I'll disappoint people if I quit.

Dinner conversations revolve around the millennial and Gen-Z terms "anxiety," "borderline personality disorder," and "triggered," and we have to agree, despite our derision of their overuse, that people of a certain age are suffering from certain experiences unknown to us that deserve new terminology. I would always rather be in a conversation than listening to a podcast, but I must listen to every episode of the podcasts made by my friends. There is a manageable amount now, and I've only read the manuscripts of three friends who wrote books about themselves so far, and I liked the feeling of guessing who the characters with changed names were, although mostly I just thought it would be better if the names were real.

When I read the book by someone who doesn't like me about her own life, I was fascinated by her description of me, and also by her, and also by the way she promoted herself and her book. In interviews I of course read, searching for another mention of myself or of someone I know, she decided she was very brave for writing about real events, blinded by urgency to the ways it might offend real people. I wondered who it offended, since everything is so abstracted. Bitterly, I thought that she was not brave at all. I'm not naming any names either, to be clear.

My boyfriend and I saw a movie with one of the stars I'd interviewed for a magazine once. I hardly remembered speaking with her. "She's Elvis's granddaughter. She was promoting a TV show in which she plays an escort," I said.

In similar discussions, I'd said, "I interviewed her/him" about John Cale, Glenn Danzig, Jena Malone, Laura Dern, Colin Farrell, Annabella Lwin, AF Vandevorst, Christina Ricci, Yorgos Lanthimos, Sarah Silverman, Nick Jonas, Anton Yelchin, Walter Van Beirendonck, Junglepussy, BJ the Chicago Kid, Olivia Cooke, Krewella, Alice Bag, Karl Glusman, Donita Sparks, Kali Uchis, Bebe Rexha, Tove Lo, Cam'ron, Melissa Auf der Maur, Lynne Tillman, Dita Von Teese, Urs Fischer, Barbie, Terry Castle, Linda Ramone, Marilyn Manson, and so many blonde models (Paige Reifler, Stella Maxwell, Hailey Baldwin, etc). And I'd said that I'd moderated interviews with Gigi and Bella Hadid, China Machado, Selena Gomez, James Franco, Sean Avery, Courtney Love, and Lana Del Rey. And that I'd facilitated photoshoots with Kembra Pfahler, Dan Graham, Lydia Lunch, Martin Rev, Thurston Moore, Molly Ringwald, Tama Janowitz, Richard Hell, Pat Place, and James Chance.

Those were just the ones that came up naturally in conversation, though. There were so many others that no one has heard of yet or since and that I can't remember now. Mostly there wasn't a good story to go with the anecdotes. The subjects were either very used to getting interviewed, or they were not especially interesting to talk to, their interesting qualities being their collaborative projects, or they were not especially interested in talking to me. Anyway, I didn't become friends with any of them.

I interviewed Chloë Sevigny at Veselka in the East Village. She was friendly and unpretentious, and when she learned we had friends in common, she invited me to a party and chose to ride the train with me when we left, even opening her mail in front of me.

When the interview came out, it was reduced to a Q&A: basically a transcript of our conversation, edited for length, basically all gossip, which I always loved about her. One line was picked up by tabloids. She'd said she found the media presence of a young actress annoyingly vulgar. I thought that part was great.

I was standing in front of a bar in the Lower East Side one night when she walked up to me, flanked by Kim Gordon and Lizzi Bougatsos. I smiled, thinking we were friends now. She hissed, "You threw me under the bus," then turned to enter the bar next door before I could stutter my response. The women on either side of her laughed at my pained expression and followed her. I told our mutual friend about it, who happened to be in the bar I then entered. "You'll learn from this," she said.

The experience had a surprisingly deep effect on me, it's true. I didn't want to apologize, but I didn't want to defend my industry, either. What I didn't understand was that if Chloë didn't like the coverage of her slight, why had she said it. When I see her around New York, I avoid her path, even though I'm sure she's over it, this total non-event in the grand scheme of her life, a life I consider a truly compelling and genuine expression of cinematic form. No one has a career like hers. I still think she is very cool, but I didn't for a while after that exchange.

"Do you ever want to do that sort of thing again?" My boyfriend asked me, about interviewing celebrities. I said I had no interest at all, although I still loved them and I loved finding out about their lives. It was because I loved them that I didn't want to keep meeting them, I said. A famous white rapper once got my number and tried to meet up with me late at night, I said, and it meant nothing to me because I knew he just wanted to be interviewed.

To be invited to something as someone other than press, I said, was the best feeling, after being invited to so many things as that, although I did sort of miss the invitations. I'd turned so many down, they stopped coming as frequently. What I had to remember was that the reason I didn't like doing these things was that I was too sensitive for them: when you meet up with a celebrity it feels like a date, except you know that for them it's an obligation.

My boyfriend and I got in a huge fight in the Lower East Side. While it was happening, I had the thought: it feels like this has happened before. I yelled that he lied, and two pretty women walking past asked me if I was okay. Not if we were okay, just me, "Girly, are you sure?" Looking out for domestic abuse. I said I was fine, but thank you. I wanted to thank them again. This was more than he could handle and he walked back to his apartment, which started multiple phone calls and hang-ups and tired texts and finally I was back at the bar having a drink alone and a older man tried to buy me another drink. I said I was leaving and he ordered me to put his number in my phone, which I did, and then he ordered me to text him, which I didn't.

Outside the bar, a guy screamed my name like we were best friends and he had forgotten to tell me he was in town. He also ordered me to put his number in my phone, which I did, and I texted him, but had no idea what his name was, since I'd only met him once before, probably ten years ago, while sharing cocaine in an apartment, I don't remember why.

I was so completely in love and heartbroken thinking that maybe it wasn't the last time I would be. I remembered being alone on my roof in the summer, single, and enjoying it. Had I enjoyed it, or had I taken photos of myself to feel distracted? I could be alone again, I thought, as long as I didn't know that's what I was.

Acknowledgments

Earlier versions of these works were first published in the following places:

"Cafeteria." In *Spike Art Quarterly*, Autumn 2016.
"Two Stops." In *n+1*, Spring 2018.
"Consulting." In *Intersubjectivity Volume II*, edited by Lou Cantor and Katherine Rochester. Germany: Sternberg Press, 2018.
"Press Release." In *Flash Art International*, Summer 2016.
"Internet as Horror." In *Sleek*, Summer 2018.
"Sever-Year Itch." In *Riot of Perfume*, 2011.
"Bellwether Boots." On affidavit.art, May 8, 2017.
"Fashion Film." In Texte Zur Kunst, Summer 2016.
"Good-looking People." On dismagazine.com, February 26, 2014.
"The Micro-trend." In The Present in Drag, edited by DIS and the Berlin Biennale. Germany: Distanz, 2016.
"The Scammer." On dismagazine.com, December 20, 2011.
"The Eighties." In *Spike Art Quarterly*, Autumn 2018.
"Thonging." On dismagazine.com, September 20, 2011.
"Confidence." In *Dazed & Confused*, Autumn 2015.
"Aspiration." In *The Destroyer*, 2011.
"Notoriety." On ssense.com, February 16, 2017.
"Legacy." In *Dazed & Confused*, Winter 2015.
"The Drop." On vmagazine.com, October 2, 2013.

"Safeway." In *Animal Shelter*, Spring 2018.
"Out of State." Serialized on spikeartmagazine.com, Summer 2017 and Summer 2018.
"Naming Names." In *New Scenario*, Summer 2018.

Thank you to the editors:

Grace Banks, Paul Barsch, Christopher Bartley, Thom Bettridge, Hunter Braithwaite, Isabella Burley, Caroline Busta, Steven Chaiken, Solomon Chase, Eugenie Dalland, Claire Marie Healy, Tilman Hornig, Marvin Jordan, Hedi El Kholti, Chris Kraus, Drew Krewer, Mark Krotov, Lou Cantor, Maureen McHugh, Kaitlin Phillips, Katherine Rochester, Lauren Roso, Marco Roso, Legacy Russell, Patrik Sandberg, Laura Schleussner, Robert Schulte, Emily Segal, David Toro, Dayna Tortorici, and Janique Vigier.

.

Natasha Stagg is the author of the novel *Surveys* published by Semiotext(e) in 2016.